《请投我一票》

A Level中文电影学习指导系列

Please Vote for Me
A Level Chinese Film Study Series

常青圖書　Cypress Books

Please Vote for Me – A Level Chinese Film Study Series

Weichi Wen, Yenchiao Fang

Editor: Xue Mei
Commissioning editor: Chengqian Guo
English proofreader: Suzanne Cummings
Advisor: Xiaohong Zhou
Cover design: Beijing Wutongying Computer Technology Co., Ltd
Layout design: Beijing Wutongying Computer Technology Co., Ltd

First published in Great Britain in 2024 by Cypress Book Co. (U.K.) Ltd.
Unit 6, Provident Industrial Estate
Pump Lane, Hayes
London UB3 3NE
United Kingdom
Tel: 0044 (0)20 88481500
E-mail: info@cypressbooks.com

Find us at www.cypressbooks.com

ISBN: 978-1-84570-047-8

Printed in China 2024

The design of this book follows the latest specification of Pearson Edexcel Level 3 Advanced GCE in Chinese (spoken Mandarin/spoken Cantonese) (9CN0). It offers learners opportunities to not only develop their understanding of the historical and social contexts of China and the film, but also to enhance their language skills. Covering topics from the one-child policy to school bullying, learners can explore various themes related to the film before delving into the film study. This resource also aims to assist teachers in lesson planning, by providing a variety of language activities that support a structured learning sequence. Learners need to master relevant vocabulary and sentence structures to produce comprehensive output and are encouraged to use an online dictionary to look up unfamiliar words or phrases to enhance independent learning. The following features are incorporated into the activities throughout this book to build language skills:

1. Vocabulary building and consolidation:

- Bold words in texts: These words are core vocabulary that we recommend students learn and master for their A Level examination. We recycle the vocabulary throughout the study guide, allowing learners to see how the words are used in the context.

- Unit vocabulary sheet: Each unit is provided with a vocabulary sheet at the back of the book, which can be used before the start of each unit to assess learners' knowledge or as a plenary activity.

2. Parts of speech learning: Understanding parts of speech is crucial for improving accuracy in sentence formation.

3. Grammar and structures practice: Essential and designated grammatical structures are provided to assist learners in composing their answers. This facilitates meaningful communication within tasks and helps achieve the objectives of each unit.

4. Advanced expressions learning: To engage advanced learners, this guide incorporates idioms and sophisticated expressions, along with alternative expressions.

5. Extension tasks: Extension tasks are available throughout the book with instructions in Chinese for capable learners.

Guides for Each Chapter

Chapter 2 Social and Historical Background Pages: p9-p30

This chapter comprises nine units designed to help learners understand the social situation in China and their relation to the film. Each unit includes a pre-reading discussion, reading comprehension exercises, and research questions related to the topic. These components are instrumental in providing learners with a comprehensive understanding of each topic, while simultaneously enhancing their research skills.

	Unit	The objective of each unit
1	导演陈为军和纪录片《请投我一票》	To learn about the director's background and the original concepts behind the creation of *Please Vote for Me*.
2	武汉	To explore the city of Wuhan and understand its modernisation process.
3	中国的小学和爱国主义教育	To understand the Chinese primary school system and its patriotic education.
4	官二代与富二代	To comprehend the social roles and dynamics of "second-generation officials" and "second-generation wealthy" in China.
5	校园霸凌	To explore the impact of school bullying on students and discuss strategies for its prevention.
6	独生子女	To discuss the history and effects of China's one-child policy and to understand its current population policy.
7	中国的政治制度	To discuss the structure and characteristics of the Chinese political system.
8	前国家主席胡锦涛	To understand who Hu Jintao is and explore his contributions to China.
9	习近平与打击贪污贿赂	To learn about Xi Jinping's anti-corruption campaign and its significance in Chinese politics.

Chapter 3 Summary and Scene Analysis Pages: p31-p72

This chapter comprises eleven units. Before beginning each unit, it is recommended that learners watch the corresponding film section by scanning the provided QR code. Each unit includes a summary, and an analysis of key scenes, along with practice in vocabulary, grammar or sentence structures. This chapter aims to deepen learners' understanding of the key events in each section of the film, while also focusing on teaching relevant cinematic vocabulary and key structures. Extension tasks are provided for more challenges.

	Unit	The objective of each unit
1	什么是民主？	To describe key scenes at the start of the film and during the flag-raising ceremony.
2	三位候选人	To identify key camara shorts and how the director introduces the main characters and the classroom setting.
3	三位候选人与他们的家庭	To compare the differing personalities and attitudes of the three candidates after being selected as class monitor candidates.
4	"打倒晓菲"事件	To discuss what happened in the "Down with Xiaofei" incident and how it occurred.
5	成成的才艺秀	To observe Cheng Cheng's tactics for his talent show and identify key scenes.
6	现任班长的忧虑	To compare Luo Lei's performance with the other two candidates and discuss his reasons for considering withdrawal from the election.
7	罗雷父母献计——轻轨之旅	To identify reasons why Luo Lei regains his popularity among his classmates.
8	成成与晓菲的辩论赛	To compare the approaches of Cheng Cheng's parents and Xiaofei's mother in preparing their children for the debate, and to compare the candidates' performances.
9	罗雷与成成的辩论赛	To compare how the parents of Luo Lei and Cheng Cheng prepare for their children's debate and evaluate the three candidates' performances in debating.
10	三位候选人的最后冲刺	To discuss the family activities of the three candidates before the final speech and to analyse their reactions.
11	投票开始与结果公布	To discuss the outcome of the election, students' reflections, and strategies to support a peaceful and fair class monitor election in the future.

To boost students' listening skills, a link to the video without English subtitles is also accessible by scanning the QR code on the right. There are more details shown in this version of the film, especially for Chapter 3: Units 3, 6 and 7.

Chapter 4 Characters Analysis

Pages: p73-p130

The aim of this chapter is to focus on the analysis of both main and minor characters. Each unit begins with an English introduction of each character, followed by a presentation task. Learners are encouraged to highlight key points in the English introduction and then complete the accompanying table. For more capable learners, it is recommended to complete the table in Chinese using the provided structures. To gain a comprehensive understanding of each character, there are problem-solving activities such as gap-filling exercises, identifying false descriptions, and translation tasks. Identifying key quotes and describing their key scenes with the suggested idioms helps consolidate understanding of each character and learn how to use the idioms in the context.

	Unit	The objective of each unit
1	主角分析：许晓菲	To gain a deeper understanding of Xiaofei's strengths and weaknesses and her relationship with her mum.
2	主角分析：成成	To analyse Cheng Cheng's behaviour during the election, focusing on his interactions with other students.
3	主角分析：罗雷	To explore how Luo Lei won the election and his leadership style as the current class monitor.
4	配角分析：张老师	To explore Mrs. Zhang's role as a homeroom teacher and how she supports this election.
5	配角分析：晓菲妈妈	To understand the role and influence of Xiaofei's mum in this election.
6	配角分析：罗雷父母	To discover how Luo Lei's parents interfere in this election and its impacts.
7	配角分析：成成的妈妈与继父	To learn how Cheng Cheng's parents encourage and support Cheng Cheng throughout the election process.

Chapter 5 Essay Practice Pages: p131-p134

This chapter includes a list of essay practice questions, accompanied by writing guidance in both Chinese and English. Learners are encouraged to use the provided checklist both before and during their writing process to ensure the essay's thoroughness and clarity. They are expected to respond critically and analytically to each question. For additional support, guided questions for each essay are available in the appendices.

编写理念 Writing Philosophy

To address the teaching and learning needs of the Chinese A Level studies, we have identified a significant gap: the absence of a comprehensive, easy-to-understand, and practical reference book specifically for the writing paper. This realisation inspired us to create a study guide tailored for A Level film studies. *Please Vote for Me*, a film considered highly accessible, has been chosen for its suitability for non-native English students learning in the UK. Our goal is to fill this gap by providing a valuable resource for both front-line teachers and students. We believe that this book will become an essential tool for A Level students, yielding long-term benefits for both the academic and educational communities.

教材体系 Textbook System

This comprehensive film study guide is designed for students preparing for their A Level exam: film essays, specifically tailored to enhance the understanding of the captivating film *Please Vote for Me*. Ideal for learners who have reached HSK 3-4 proficiency or have successfully completed their Chinese GCSE Higher tier examination, this guide delves deep into the analysis of the film, employing essential vocabulary and grammatical structures that range from HSK levels 5 to 6.

Written to cater to the needs of advanced learners, this book offers a unique blend of language-focused challenges and cultural exploration. Its content not only aligns with A Level standards but also provides an immersive learning experience. Whether you are a student aiming to enhance your Mandarin or a Chinese film enthusiast keen on exploring Chinese culture, this guide serves as an essential resource. It helps you understand and appreciate *Please Vote for Me* in its full cultural and linguistic context.

作者简介 About the Authors

Weichi Wen completed her PGCE programme at Goldsmiths, University of London, and has taught in both state and independent settings in the UK. She has gained extensive experience in teaching students learning Chinese as a foreign language and bilingual students throughout her teaching career, which includes 9 years of teaching CIE Chinese Pre-U film studies.

Yenchiao Fang graduated with an MED in Education from the University of Bristol before pursuing a PGCE at the UCL Institute of Education. His teaching experience encompasses a range of educational settings, including state and independent, primary and secondary schools both in China and the UK.

致谢 Acknowledgements

I would like to express my heartfelt gratitude to my family for their support and encouragement throughout the process. I am also deeply grateful to Putney High School, which has nurtured my passion for teaching, alongside my supportive MFL colleagues.

— Weichi

I would like to thank all the family and friends who have provided invaluable advice and support throughout my writing journey. Additionally, I extend my gratitude to our editors for their patience and feedback on our work.

— Yenchiao

Lastly, we wish to express our profound gratitude to Xiaohong Zhou (advisor), Victor W, Tony C, and our Mandarin teacher colleagues, particularly in the Trinity Hotpot Group. Additionally, we extend a heartfelt thank you to our publisher Cypress Books, for granting us with this remarkable publishing opportunity and to Sophie for her patience and exceptional support.

目 录
CONTENTS

Chapter 4 Characters Analysis 73

Chapter 5 Essay Practice 131

Appendix I Guidance for Chapter 5 Essay Questions 135

Appendix II Vocabulary 140

Chapter

1

Introduction

《请投我一票》(*Please Vote for Me*) is an award-winning documentary directed by Chen Weijun and is part of the international documentary project "Why Democracy?" in 2007, which comprises ten films exploring various aspects of democracy. The film follows a unique democratic experiment taking place in a third-grade classroom at Evergreen Elementary School in Wuhan, a city of similar size to London and the largest in central China. The students, all approximately eight years old, are given the opportunity to elect a class monitor, a role traditionally assigned by the teacher, who holds significant authority over the students' order and discipline. This marks the first time that students at this school have been granted the chance to vote for their class monitor.

Director Chen Weijun begins by asking an eight-year-old Chinese girl, "what is democracy?" She does not respond. Then he asks, "what is a vote?". Instead of responding, the next little girl squirms. Later, Mrs. Zhang, the class teacher, briefly defines democracy to the class and gives examples, explaining to her students that they will try something new this semester. The students show no knowledge or experience of democracy. She further announces that a group of teachers has selected three candidates who will campaign for the position in a simulated democratic election. Luo Lei, the current monitor with two years of experience, is confident in his ability to continue leading the classroom and runs his own campaign. The primary challenger, Cheng Cheng, is motivated by a desire for power and the ability to boss other students around. The female candidate, Xu Xiaofei, who is shy and lacks confidence, is excited to be nominated and primarily campaigns with other female friends to secure votes. Each candidate is supported by two campaign assistants. The parents of the candidates do everything they can to help their children win. Although Mrs. Zhang explains at the beginning of the election that "democracy" means "people being their own masters" (everyone has the right to express their opinion, and the class monitor is chosen by the entire class), the film seems to argue the opposite. It attempts to use the campaigns of the three candidates to suggest that all democratic processes are questionable.

The three candidates must take part in three events to showcase their suitability for the role of class monitor during their campaign. The first event is a talent show, where each candidate performs or sings a musical piece. The second event is a class debate, where the candidates emphasise their qualifications and critique their opponents' weaknesses. The final event is a speech in which each candidate addresses their classmates and appeals for their votes.

On the first day of the talent show, Xiaofei is the first to perform, despite seemingly having received the least stage preparation at home. She quickly falls apart when Cheng Cheng, Luo Lei, and others resort to dirty tricks, heckling her during her performance. The teacher consoles Xiaofei and reprimands the disruptive students. Then Cheng Cheng apologises to Xiaofei for Luo Lei and requests that Luo Lei also apologise; however, he fails to mention his role in planning with his assistant to cause this chaos. Overcome with emotion, Xiaofei returns to the stage and continues playing the flute while sobbing.

Cheng Cheng is the second performer. He delivers a stellar performance and is an excellent orator, adept at capturing the students' attention. After he sings, his classmates applaud him as if he were a celebrity. He even interacts with other classmates after the song to make him seem like he would be a friendly and an approachable leader. Cheng Cheng's mother works in a television station, and he regularly undergoes practise sessions with her for both his performance and speeches.

Cheng Cheng covertly encourages Xiaofei to taunt Luo Lei on the second day of the talent show, before Luo Lei's performance. From the wings, Cheng Cheng shouts, "out of tune!" as Luo Lei takes the stage to play the flute and sing. Cheng Cheng and Luo Lei engage in a heated exchange after the performance. Subsequently, some students are interviewed and asked to declare their support for a candidate. At this juncture, Luo Lei abruptly announces his withdrawal from the election.

Cheng Cheng continues campaigning for votes, promising some classmates that if they vote for him, he will appoint them as deputy class monitor or committee members. Luo Lei's parents (his mother works as a police officer, and his father is the department's director), are worried about the election after hearing that the talent show did not go well. His father suggests taking the class on the monorail, the city's latest mode of transportation, stating that it will foster friendship and unity. Although Luo Lei initially refuses any assistance from his parents with the election, he looks quite relieved after hearing their plan. This free outing greatly enhances Luo Lei's popularity. Consequently, Cheng Cheng informs his teacher of his intention to withdraw from the election because he feels that his popularity has dramatically declined after the monorail trip. His mother disapproves of him quitting, and his teacher encourages him not to give up.

Before the upcoming debate, Xiaofei's mother (a single mother working as a school administrator), boosts her daughter's confidence during a tour and advises her to take note of the weaknesses of the other two candidates. Cheng Cheng is also discreetly compiling a list of Xiaofei and Luo Lei's weaknesses. His mother is pleased to see her son grow and develop competitive skills.

The first debate pits Cheng Cheng against Xiaofei. On stage, the two candidates highlight and defend each other's flaws. The articulate Cheng Cheng leaves Xiaofei speechless in this event, after her weakness exposed in the talent show. Cheng Cheng, who performs strongly in the debate and seems to have the upper hand, even requests that the director interviews the same female classmate twice, to determine whether if she truly intends to vote for him. Cheng Cheng suspects that the female student is lying when she claims she chose him simply because he was nearby.

The second round features Cheng Cheng going up against Luo Lei. Cheng Cheng conducts interviews with his classmates to uncover Luo Lei's weaknesses, such as his tendency to engage in physical altercations. The parents of both candidates remain involved in the election: Luo Lei's father instructs his son on how to manipulate others and advises him to remain composed and respond logically, while Cheng Cheng's mother coaches her son on effective communication and helps him prepare arguments, such as the significance of being a leader rather than a dictator in the classroom.

When the debate between Cheng Cheng and Luo Lei commences the following day, Cheng Cheng confidently recites the class management principles he has learned from his parents, adopting a mature tone. He highlights his intention to be a leader rather than a dictator. To support his statements, he asks his classmates to raise their hands if they have been physically harmed by Luo Lei. In response, Luo Lei questions Cheng Cheng on whom he would vote for if given the chance. Cheng Cheng pauses briefly before responding, "I would vote for myself." At this moment, Luo Lei erupts in anger, accusing Cheng Cheng of deceitfulness. He points to the school motto, "Honesty and Courage" displayed above the blackboard, and claims that Cheng Cheng privately expressed his intention to vote for Luo Lei but is now proclaiming his own candidacy publicly. This revelation leaves Cheng Cheng speechless. Outside the classroom, Luo Lei's father gives a thumbs-up in appreciation of his son's performance. Cheng Cheng then brings up Luo Lei's inclination for physical aggression, prompting Luo Lei to promise to make changes.

The final event preceding the vote is the candidates' speeches, with parental assistance once again. Xiaofei's speech is written by her mother based on their usual conversations, making it more closely related to her life experiences. Cheng Cheng's parents provide him with a revised speech, after realising the language that his stepfather used is too mature for children to understand. Cheng Cheng and Luo Lei's parents instruct them on appropriate hand-raising and bowing techniques. Luo Lei's father informs his son of the upcoming Mid-Autumn Festival and their preparations of delightful little gifts (festive cards) for him to distribute to his classmates after the speech. Following his father's guidance,

Luo Lei instructs his assistants to distribute the small gift cards immediately after his speech. Mrs. Zhang proceeds to distribute the ballots and reminds the students to consider their choices.

The vote concluded with Luo Lei winning the position of class monitor by a significant majority of votes (25), Xiaofei received 6 votes, and Cheng Cheng received 8. With a triumphant expression, Luo Lei proudly raises a sign that reads "Class Leader". Both Cheng Cheng and Xiaofei shed tears as they were not selected as class monitors. The class teacher summarises the election process and requests Xiaofei, Cheng Cheng, and Luo Lei to shake hands.

The film documents the children's journey throughout the campaign, both within the school premises and their homes. The candidates' parents provide encouragement and support as they practise and commit speeches for each phase of the campaign. Nevertheless, the pressure remains intense, resulting in tears and occasional outbursts of anger. At school, the candidates engage in one-on-one conversations with their fellow classmates, making promises, strategising (including resorting to negative tactics), and occasionally expressing doubts about their own chances of winning. The film leaves it to the viewers to decide the level of "success" achieved by this democratic experiment and its implications on democracy education in China. It urges those devoted to promoting democracy in China to contemplate the feasibility and processes involved in its implementation.

THINKING MORE DEEPLY

- The children at the beginning of the film were unable to define democracy. Do you think the children in your country would have trouble coming up with a definition? What is your definition of democracy?

- What are your thoughts on how these three candidates were chosen to participate in this election? Do you think it's fair?

- Do you agree that the three stages (Talent Show, Debate, and Speech) that the candidates were asked to participate in for this class monitor election were reasonable and fair? Please explain.

- Were you surprised by any of the behaviour exhibited by the children, including anything the children said or by the way they expressed themselves? Please explain.

- Have you experienced class elections in school? What do you think the similarities and differences would be between how the children in the film and the children in your country campaign for election?

- How do you feel about the parents in the film and the ways they assisted their children in campaigning? Would the parents in your country provide similar support to their children? What actions might they take differently?

- Are you content with the outcome of the class monitor election? Why or why not?

- Are you satisfied with the way the class teacher in the film handled this election? If you were Mrs. Zhang, how would you lead your class in a democratic election?

- In your opinion, did the class monitor election function as an exercise in democracy? What do you believe the children gained from this experience? What did you learn from this experiment?

Chapter

2

Social and Historical Background

UNIT 1

导演陈为军和纪录片《请投我一票》

Pre-reading discussion

▶ 1 Why did Chen Weijun decide to create the documentary *Please Vote for Me*, and what social and educational issues does it address?

▶ 2 What distinctions can be made between shooting a documentary and shooting a fictional film?

▶ 3 How did the public respond to *Please Vote for Me*?

tí cái = 主题

陈为军是中国**著名**的**纪录片导演**。**由于**他的作品有出色的**摄影技巧**和对**社会**问题的深入**探讨**，因此**近年来受**到广泛的**关注**。他的**作品主题大多来自**不同的社会**题材**，**例如**环境保护、历史文化、社会**现实**等。"**尊重生命**"一直是陈导演**拍摄**每一部纪录片的**中心思想**。他的每一部作品都**表现出**他对生命的尊重，对人权的关注，以及对社会的**强烈责任感**。

陈为军最著名的作品之一是 2007 年拍摄的纪录片《请投我一票》，它**真实**地记录了三位中国小学生**竞选班长**的**过程**。除了入围奥斯卡（Oscars）最佳纪录长片单元，本片还**获得**了亚什兰独立电影节（Ashland Independent Film Festival）最佳纪录片**奖**。

至于为什么想拍摄这部纪录片呢？那是因为一个**偶然**的**机会**，陈为军导演问了**同事**的孩子成成一个问题：老师、商人、**领导**，你长大以后想当哪个？成成想都没想就说想当领导。成成的理由是，老师每天**批改**作业很**辛苦**，而商人做生意可能会**失败**。**于是**陈导演做了一个**调查**，**发现**大多数朋友的孩子都想当领导。他开始**感到**疑惑：为什么周遭孩子们的志向不是从事其他**职业**呢？因此他**决定**拍摄这部纪录片，找出**原因**。

在这部纪录片中，陈导演的拍摄**手法**让观众**感受**到孩子们**激烈**且真实的**选举**过程。纪录片所**呈现**的社会和**教育**问题让社会**大众**有机会**了解**身教、言教、境教对孩子教育的重要性。

Activity 1 Put an X next to the correct statements. (There are four correct statements.)

A	导演陈为军是中国著名的作家。
B	导演陈为军喜欢用纪录片的方式探讨社会问题。
C	导演陈为军的作品表达出他对生命的尊重。
D	《请投我一票》是导演陈为军在 2007 年制作的一部动画片。
E	导演陈为军拍摄《请投我一票》是因为他自己小时候也想当班长。
F	《请投我一票》入围了亚什兰独立电影节最佳纪录片奖。
G	导演陈为军拍摄《请投我一票》是为了探讨为什么做老师很辛苦。
H	导演陈为军以前不了解为什么很多朋友的孩子都想做领导。
I	《请投我一票》让大家了解到大人的言行对小孩子的影响。

Activity 2 Answer the following questions in Chinese or English.

1 陈为军是拍什么的著名导演？

由于他很好的摄摄系影技巧和对社会问题的探讨

2 陈为军在 2007 年拍摄的作品是什么？

请投我一颗票

3 陈为军发现大多数朋友的孩子想做什么工作？

领导

4 从纪录片里真实的选举过程中，社会大众可以了解到什么的重要性？

身教、言教、境教对孩子的教育

Activity 3 Prepare a presentation on one of the following questions and deliver it to your class.

1 为什么导演陈为军选择用拍纪录片的方式来探讨社会问题？

2 陈导演还有其他哪些有名的作品？

3 纪录片《请投我一票》是如何体现中国社会中的民主意义的？

4 为什么大人的"身教、言教、境教"对小孩子的教育很重要？

UNIT 2 武汉

Pre-reading discussion

▸ **1** Where is Wuhan located in China?

▸ **2** Wuhan is a city abundant in Chinese history. What are some renowned attractions there?

▸ **3** How do you believe the swift development of Wuhan's infrastructure might impact the city's cultural heritage and traditions?

《请投我一票》是 2007 年由陈为军导演在武汉常青第一小学拍摄的纪录片。武汉，位于中国的中部地区，有"九省通衢"（指交通便利，地理位置很重要）的美誉，同时也是一个**拥有丰富**历史文化的古城。武汉夏季长且炎热，降雨量也**比较**充足。

武汉被认为是中国中西部地区的科技、教育、**金融中心**，拥有多所著名的**高等学校**，如武汉大学、华中科技大学等。为了跟上 21 **世纪**初中国**经济**的快速**发展**，武汉近年来**进行**了重要的城市改造。

在交通**方面**，武汉**拥有完整**的公路、**铁路**和民航**网络**，是全国重要的**运输**中心。近年来，新的**高架**公路和地铁**路线**也如期**完工**。**除此以外**，人们在这里也可以**使用**许多新的**公共交通工具**，例如更**智能**、更环保的**电动**公交车、**轻轨**等。

陈为军拍摄纪录片的时候，轻轨在武汉是一项最**现代**的交通工具，所以当罗雷的**父母**带全班去**乘坐**轻轨时，我们可以看到小朋友的脸上**流露出**既期待又**兴奋**的**表情**。

Activity 1 **Answer the following questions in Chinese or English.**

1 《请投我一票》的拍摄地点在武汉的哪里？

_____

2 武汉的天气有什么特点？（写出两点）

_____

3 近年来，武汉有哪些基础建设完工？（写出两点）

_____

4 武汉有哪些新的公共交通工具？（写出两点）

_____

5 纪录片中，在乘坐轻轨时，小朋友的心情如何？

_____

中国的小学和爱国主义教育

Pre-reading discussion

▶ 1 Why is it a common practice for students to collectively read aloud texts in Chinese school?

▶ 2 What does it mean by patriotic education?

▶ 3 In what ways do schools in China work to cultivate students' love and responsibility for their country through daily routines and educational practices?

　　小学教育是中国义务教育的**基础**，也是**培养**学生**学习**兴趣的重要阶段，一共六年。在这六年里，学生要学习语文、数学、科学、道德与法制等基础**知识**。除此以外，不少学生也会**通过**上书法、绘画、音乐、体育等**课程**来培养不同的兴趣和**技能**。

　　近年来，中国的小学教育开始**注重提升**学生的**创新能力**、**批判性思维**和**团队合作**能力。**学校**通常会**尽力**为学生**提供**丰富的学习**资源**和**多元化**的学习环境。老师们常常**鼓励**学生参加各种各样的课外活动。**家长**们在家也会**积极**地给孩子**支持**和**辅导**，有时**甚至**会**安排**课后的**才艺班**或辅导课。

　　在中国的小学课程中，语文是最重要的科目**之一**，注重提升学生**表达**和**写作**的能力。例如，在《请投我一票》的一个教室**场景**中，我们可以看到全班学生在语文课上一起大声地读一篇**关于**如何**演讲**的**文章**。

　　爱国主义教育在中国的小学也备受**重视**。在过去，红领巾被**认为**是中国革命文化的**一部分**，也是中国共青团的**标志**。红领巾不仅**代表勇敢**，而且**象征**着中国近代**伟大**的革命历史，因此学校通过让学生**佩戴**红领巾来培养学生的爱国**意识**。从影片中我们可以**观察**到全校学生在参加早上的升旗仪式时都会**自觉**佩戴红领巾，来**表现**爱国的**精神**。

　　通过这些日常的**细节**和教育实践，中国的小学成功培养了学生的爱国**情感**和责任感。

Activity 1 **Answer the following questions in Chinese or English.**

1. 中国小学的义务教育一共有多少年？

2. 近年来，除了基础知识，中国的小学教育还开始提升学生的哪些能力？（写出两点）

3. 中国的父母通常会如何帮助孩子发展？（写出两点）

4. 中国小学语文课的教学重点是什么？（写出两点）

5. 中国小学生在升旗仪式时，通过佩戴什么来表现爱国精神？

Activity 2 **Prepare a presentation on one of the following questions and deliver it to your class.**

1. 近年来，中国的小学通过什么方式来提升学生的创新能力、批判性思维和团队合作能力？

2. 中国的教育系统和考试与你国家的有什么异同？

3. 中国政府在 2023 年通过了《中华人民共和国爱国主义教育法》，从 2024 年元旦开始实施，目的是通过加强中国人的爱国教育来提升人民的民族精神和团结精神。为什么这样的法律（law）对一个国家的安全和发展很重要呢？

官二代与富二代

Pre-reading discussion

▶ 1 How can parents' social status and connections influence their children's opportunities?

▶ 2 Privilege can play a significant role in many societies, not just in China. Can you think of examples from other cultures or contexts?

▶ 3 How can people ensure that a democratic election can take place in a fair setting, considering candidates with vastly different resources and backgrounds?

　　"官二代"是指官员**家庭**的第二代，也就是父母是官员的人；**富有**人家的孩子在社会上常常被称为"富二代"。**一般来说**，"官二代"和"富二代"在社会上往往能获得比普通家庭孩子更好的**生活水平**和教育机会。

　　由于"官二代"和"富二代"的父母往往有较高的社会**地位**和较多的**财富**，在**某些情况**下，他们可能有机会通过父母的**关系**获得一些"特权"，从中**得到**更多的资源和**优势**，因此他们可能在**人生**道路上会比一般人更容易**取得**成功。不过不可否认的是，也有不少"官二代"和"富二代"不依靠自己的家庭**背景**，而是通过自身的努力和奋斗获得成功，**并**积极地关怀社会，为**国家**做贡献。

　　纪录片《请投我一票》**展现**了罗雷的警察父母**利用工作单位**的"特权"，使用一些**方法**帮助罗雷赢得班长选举的过程。比如，他们给罗雷班上的同学安排了一次轻轨旅行，**提高**了同学们对罗雷的好感与支持度。在罗雷与成成**辩论**之前，罗雷的父母**准备**了一些**重点**问题，**训练**罗雷演讲，教他**如何**应答。罗雷爸爸甚至亲自到学校观看辩论的过程，并为**所有**同学准备了中秋节卡片。我们可以看到罗雷的父母　倾尽全力　，为的就是让他们的儿子赢得班长选举。在这种家庭背景下长大的罗雷，**面对**同学时特别有自信。

　　相比之下，许晓菲与罗雷的性格就有着　天壤之别　了。晓菲来自一个**单亲**家庭，她的**性格内向**、安静，对自己没有什么自信，也没什么主见，总是等妈妈给她提供**意见**。在影片的**访谈**中，晓菲的妈妈感到家里**条件**不足，比起罗雷家的优势，她**觉得**自己**无法**给晓菲提供像罗雷父母一样的帮助。

无论是因为前任班长身份的优势还是父母提供的资源，罗雷最后都赢得了班长选举。每一张选票都带着一种**期望**：罗雷能证明自己是一位班级的**管理**者而不是统治者，并且对学校及同学有良好的贡献。这样的**事**不禁让人**思考**：社会公平和个人特权之间的**平衡**应该如何建立？

倾尽全力：指将所有力量、精力和资源都投入到某件事情上。

天壤之别：形容两者差别极大。

Activity 1 Choose the correct answer.

1 什么是"官二代"？
   A 华人的子女。
   B 官员的子女。
   C 工人的子女。
   D 普通人的子女。

2 拥有"特权"的人一般指什么人？
   A 财富不足的人。
   B 由于个人才华和努力而成功的人。
   C 在社会中有更多资源和优势的人。
   D 社会地位低的人。

3 为什么"官二代"和"富二代"往往比一般人更容易获得成功？
   A 因为他们往往比普通人更聪明。
   B 因为他们往往从小就当班长。
   C 因为他们往往都来自双亲家庭。
   D 因为他们往往有更好的家庭背景和机会。

4 在纪录片《请投我一票》中，罗雷的家庭与"特权"有什么关系？

    A 罗雷的父母是警察，他们利用工作单位的"特权"来安排学校旅行。

    B 罗雷的父母通过做兼职工作来获得更多的金钱和"特权"。

    C 罗雷的父母使用"特权"让张老师帮助罗雷当上班长。

    D 罗雷的父母反对使用"特权"，他们相信公平竞争。

5 罗雷的父母是如何帮助他准备辩论的？

    A 请张老师来帮他练习。

    B 教罗雷如何回答辩论问题。

    C 教罗雷如何用"气"来辩论。

    D 教罗雷在班上起哄。

6 许晓菲来自什么样的家庭？

    A 三代同堂。

    B 官员的家庭。

    C "富二代"家庭。

    D 单亲家庭。

7 许晓菲与罗雷在竞选班长的过程中有什么不同？

    A 晓菲的家庭没有罗雷的家庭有权势。

    B 跟晓菲相比，罗雷对同学说话的口气与态度有很大的不同。

    C 晓菲的性格比罗雷内向。

    D 所有选项都正确。

Activity 2 **Prepare a presentation on one of the following questions and deliver it to your class.**

1 为什么"官二代"与"富二代"往往有更好的教育资源和机会？

2 在中国，有哪些"官二代"和"富二代"对社会有良好的贡献？他们做了什么？

3 在纪录片《请投我一票》中，三位候选人分别从家庭中得到了什么帮助？

校园霸凌

Pre-reading discussion

▶ **1** What is the traditional role and authority of a class monitor in Chinese schools?

▶ **2** If you were a teacher, a principal, or an education minister, how would you handle bullying behaviour and culture in your school / country?

▶ **3** In your opinion, what responsibilities should a class monitor have, and how should they serve as role models for their classmates?

校园**霸凌**又称"校园**暴力**",它不仅会**危害**学生的身心健康,还可能对学生**未来**的**人际关系**发展**造成影响**。校园霸凌的**种类包括**语言霸凌、身体霸凌和心理霸凌等。

在中国的小学,班长是一个有着一定权力的**职位**,而在过去,甚至有班长私自处罚不听话的同学。在纪录片《请投我一票》中,现任班长罗雷认为不听话的同学就应该受到处罚,还通过打人和**骂**人的**方式使**同学服从他。在影片中的辩论环节,成成指出罗雷所展现的是一种统治者的行为,并不是领导者的行为。

根据调查,在中国有百分之七十以上的校园霸凌**事件**最后都 不了了之 。其中**主要**的原因是,有的学校没有正视校园霸凌的严重性,而是**抱着**一种漠视或大事化小、小事化了 的**处理态度**。

在纪录片中,我们看到班主任张老师并没有积极、**及时**地处理学生的霸凌行为。例如,在罗雷才艺**表演**时,成成向张老师透露:他的妈妈教了他一些对付罗雷的" 招式 zhāo shì ",但张老师听到后并没有**立刻**阻止。

不了了之:该做的事情没有做完就放在一边不管了。

大事化小,小事化了:将可能成为重大问题的事情处理得很简单,不给予过多关注。

随着学校道德教育水平的提高，现今的孩子**清楚**地明白班长应该是积极协助班主任、帮助同学的好榜样，而不是滥用权力的校园霸凌者。除此以外，老师们也应该意识到，学习如何判定及处理校园霸凌的**专业**知识是非常有必要的。

Activity 1 Put an X next to the correct statements. (There are four correct statements.)

A	校园霸凌不会对学生的心理造成影响。
B	校园霸凌不会影响学生将来交朋友。
C	班长罗雷曾经通过打人和骂人的方式让同学听他的话。
D	成成在辩论中指出罗雷不是一个领导者。
E	霸凌是家长和学生自己的问题，和学校没有关系。
F	调查显示，有的学校不愿意花时间积极地处理校园霸凌。
G	张老师及时阻止了成成对付罗雷。
H	为了协助班主任，班长可以通过打人和骂人的方式来管理班级。
I	老师们应该具备处理校园霸凌的专业知识。

Activity 2 Prepare a presentation on one of the following questions and deliver it to your class.

1 校园霸凌对学生有哪些负面影响？

2 你认为一位好班长应该拥有什么特质？

3 你认为学校的老师应该如何有效地处理校园霸凌？

4 在《请投我一票》中，你发现了哪些校园霸凌的行为？如果你是影片中的受害者，你会如何应对？

5 2023 年 12 月，台湾省台北市的一所中学发生了一起严重的校园霸凌事件，导致（cause）一名中学生在学校被割颈身亡。这起事件凸显出校园霸凌问题仍然（still）是目前需要大众关心的社会议题。根据这个事件，你认为应该如何制定法律来防止类似的事情再发生？你认为老师们在学校有权力随时检查学生的书包、确认有没有危险物品吗？

UNIT 6

独生子女

Pre-reading discussion

▶ 1 What was the primary reason for China's implementation of the one-child policy?

▶ 2 How might being an only child under this policy potentially impact the child's social experiences and emotions?

▶ 3 Despite the relaxation of the one-child policy, why have many Chinese families chosen to continue having only one child?

　　"独生子女政策"是指中国**政府**从 1980 年到 2015 年推行的**计划生育**政策——**提倡**一对**夫妇**只生育一个孩子。**目的**是在**追求**社会与经济发展的同时，**降低人口增长**所带来的**压力**，**防止**国家**面临**食物和其他资源的短缺问题，使**人民**的生活水平能得到提高。

　　然而，**长期**以来，尽管这项**措施**大大地**缓解**了中国人口增长过快的问题，但是**对于**许多家庭与整个社会来说，影响**不一定**都是积极的。因为这些独生子女要面临的**挑战**以及需要**克服**的**困难**可能会**超出**我们的**想象**。以下几点是许多**研究**调查中**提到**的。

　　第一，社交技能。由于在日常生活中**缺乏**与**兄弟姐妹**的**互动**，一些独生子女可能在与同龄人**沟通**时缺乏**经验**，**导致**社交技能比较弱。

　　第二，社交压力。由于没有兄弟姐妹的**陪伴**，独生子女可能会时常感到**孤独**和寂寞，**尤其**是在家庭**聚会**或节日期间。

　　第三，**独立**压力。独生子女往往被期望更早地学会独立，这可能给他们带来心理压力，因为他们需要在很多事情上自己做决定。

　　第四，父母期望。独生子女常常需要承受来自父母的较高期望，因为他们是家里**唯一**的希望和未来的寄托。

　　第五，**竞争**压力。在学校和工作中，独生子女可能感受到来自同龄人的激烈竞争压力，因为家人常常期望他们在学业和职业上表现优异。

第六，经济压力。独生子女在照顾年老的父母和**祖父母**时，可能会面临比较大压力，因为他们没有兄弟姐妹分担责任。例如，父母的**养老**费用等。

第七，家庭负担。独生子女成年后往往会面临同时**养育**年幼的小孩儿和照顾年老的父母的责任与压力。

此外，独生子女政策也导致中国男女人口**比例严重**失衡。由于"重男轻女""男性有 传宗接代 的责任"等传统**观念** 根深蒂固 ，许多家庭更倾向于生男孩儿，导致女性人口**数量**减少。这在一定程度上**限制**了年轻人口增长，导致人口年龄**结构**的失衡，进一步加剧了社会老龄化问题。

独生子女被**宠坏**的**镜头**在纪录片《请投我一票》中 展露无遗 。例如，成成对妈妈大呼小叫，没大没小；晓菲在生活上对妈妈极度**依赖**；罗雷以自我为中心，在学校 目中无人 ，一生气就打人、骂人。这些被宠坏的孩子又被叫作"小公主"或"小皇帝"。再比如，由于中国人一般有"望子成龙、望女成凤"的观念，我们可以看到三位小候选人的家长也在积极地帮助孩子赢得班长选举。

尽管独生子女政策已经**结束**，中国政府也从 2021 年开始施行三孩政策，在**法律**上**允许**一对夫妻生育三个孩子。然而，长达三十多年的独生子女政策**仍然**对中国社会发展有着深远的影响。

> **传宗接代**：子孙一代又一代地延续下去。
>
> **根深蒂固**：比喻基础稳固，不容易动摇。
>
> **展露无遗**：指完全展现出来。
>
> **目中无人**：形容骄傲自大，看不起别人。

Activity 1 Put an X next to the correct statements. (There are four correct statements.)

A	独生子女政策是指每个家庭至少要生一个孩子。
B	独生子女政策对中国社会的影响都是积极的。
C	独生子女没有兄弟姐妹可以互相帮助。

（续表）

D	独生子女政策导致男女人口比例失衡。
E	在中国，照顾父母不是独生子女的责任。
F	中国从来都没有重男轻女的观念。
G	独生子女在学校较少感受到来自同龄人的竞争压力。
H	"小公主"或"小皇帝"是指那些被宠坏的孩子。
I	目前中国政府实行三孩政策。

Activity 2 **Prepare a presentation on one of the following questions and deliver it to your class.**

1 独生子女政策给中国社会带来了哪些影响？

2 独生子女要面对哪些压力？为什么？

3 你认为目前中国的三孩政策会有什么影响？为什么？

4 现代中国年轻人对"生儿育女"的态度呈现怎样的趋势？为什么？

中国的政治制度

Pre-reading discussion

▸ **1** What is the CCP?

▸ **2** What is the structure of the Chinese government?

▸ **3** What is Chinese democracy?

中华人民共和国（简称"中国"）是一个由中国共产党领导的**多党**合作和**政治协商**的国家。也就是说，中国共产党是中国的唯一**执政党**。此外，还有其他八个**民主党派**。在中国共产党领导的前提下，这些民主党派拥有参政党的地位，可与执政党合作并**参与讨论**公共**事务**，**体现**为"共产党领导、多党派合作，共产党执政、多党派参政"。由此可见，中国的选举**制度**与**西方**多党制国家的**系统**不完全相同。

在这样的政治制度下，中国也拥有民主的**特色**，例如投票选举。在中国，全国人民代表大会是国家最高权力机关。此外，中国也有地方选举制度，允许公民选举地方政府官员。

在《请投我一票》中，三位小候选人是先由学校老师们讨论决定的，因此这三位小朋友才有了参与这次选举的机会。但是身为观众的我们并不知道老师们是根据什么**标准**做出的选择。

虽然我们看到班主任在黑板上写下大大的"民主"二字，但是她却没有**真正**教导学生民主投票的**意义**，在发现成成无礼的手段和罗雷的贿选行为时也没有立刻**纠正**他们。这也让观众**联想**到导演**是否**在**暗示**：民主并不是靠嘴上说说而已，而是需要公民的意识与素养、教育水平和道德**品格**达到一定标准才**能够**实现。

Activity 1 Put an X next to the correct statements. (There are four correct statements.)

	A	中国是由中国共产党领导的多党合作国家。
	B	中国共产党是中华人民共和国的唯一执政党。
	C	在中国，地方选举是不存在的。
	D	全国人民代表大会拥有最高国家权力。
	E	其他民主党派有参政权，但必须在中国共产党领导下进行。
	F	《请投我一票》中，班主任让全班同学都理解了民主投票的意义。
	G	《请投我一票》中，三位候选人是由学生们选出来的。
	H	实现民主不需要考虑国民素质和道德品格。
	I	《请投我一票》中，班主任立刻纠正了罗雷的贿选行为。

Activity 2 Prepare a presentation on one of the following questions and deliver it to your class.

1 请比较中国的民主与西方的民主有哪些异同？

2 一个良好的民主制度需要什么条件才能够实现？

3 投票与民主之间的关系是什么？

4 你是否同意《请投我一票》中三位小候选人的产生方式？请说明你的理由。

UNIT
8

前国家主席胡锦涛

Pre-reading discussion

▶ **1** Who is Hu Jintao?

▶ **2** China experienced rapid economic growth during Hu Jintao's leadership, with an average GDP growth rate of over 10%. How might such rapid economic growth impact a country's society and its citizens?

▶ **3**. How does Hu Jintao's approach to leadership and governance differ from that of his predecessors or successors in China?

　　在《请投我一票》中，成成的妈妈期望儿子**成为**像胡锦涛一样的领导。那么，谁是胡锦涛呢？

　　胡锦涛在 2005 年到 2013 年期间担任中华人民共和国的国家主席。在任期内，他进行了许多重要的**改革**，**推行**了多项发展措施，推动了中国的经济增长和社会**进步**。其中主要包括以下几点。

　　经济发展：胡锦涛担任国家主席期间是中国经济快速增长的**时期**，中国**国内**生产总值（GDP）年均**增长率**超过 10%。

　　对外关系：胡锦涛积极发展中国的对外关系，与**周边**国家开展**贸易**合作，**增强**中国在国际事务中的影响力。他提出了"**和谐世界**"的理念，倡导国家之间的**平等**与合作。

　　改革**开放**：胡锦涛在任期内推动了许多经济、政治和社会改革，包括加强农村发展和提高教育水平。

　　社会**稳定**：胡锦涛时期加强了社会稳定工作，提出了使"人民安居乐业"的政策，重视**解决**人民的**就业**、医疗、教育、住房等问题。

　　环境保护：胡锦涛提出了"节约资源、保护环境"的思想，致力于打造**可持续**发展的社会。

在《请投我一票》中，我们可以看出成成的妈妈 用心良苦，鼓励她的儿子通过这次班长选举，**体会**成为一个**优秀**领导不是一件容易的事。成为"胡锦涛"是成成的妈妈使用的一种**比喻**，她的**意思**是希望成成能成为一位对班级有贡献的管理者。

用心良苦：描述某人的用心，强调良好的出发点和努力去做某件事情。

Activity 1 Put an X next to the correct statements. (There are four correct statements.)

A	胡锦涛是中国第一任国家主席。
B	胡锦涛在中国推动了许多经济、政治和社会改革。
C	胡锦涛提倡国家之间的竞争和对抗。
D	胡锦涛不重视学校教育的发展。
E	胡锦涛提出了"全民健康保险"政策来解决人民医疗问题。
F	胡锦涛认为国家经济发展比环境保护重要。
G	胡锦涛致力于打造可持续发展的社会。
H	成成的妈妈认为成为一个好领导一点儿都不难。
I	成为"胡锦涛"是成成的妈妈使用的一种比喻。

Activity 2 Prepare a presentation on one of the following questions and deliver it to your class.

1 胡锦涛在中国经济方面做出了什么贡献？请举例说明。
2 胡锦涛在中国对外关系方面做出了什么贡献？请举例说明。
3 胡锦涛在中国社会稳定方面做出了什么贡献？请举例说明。
4 胡锦涛在中国文化政策和文化发展方面做出了什么贡献？请举例说明。

习近平与打击贪污贿赂

Pre-reading discussion

▸ 1 What bribery and corruption issues have recently been reported by the media internationally?

▸ 2 Do you believe that a fair and just election truly exists?

▸ 3 If you were a candidate in an election, would you accept support from your family to win the election? Why or why not?

贪污和贿赂都是严重的违法行为。贪污是指公职人员为了获得不正当利益，利用职权进行不诚实、甚至**犯罪**的行为。贿赂是指给予他人金钱或者其他**利益作为**交换条件，来达到特别的目的。

习近平是中国现任国家主席和中共中央总书记，从 2013 年上任以后就一直重视贪污及贿赂的问题。近年来，中国政府致力于打击贪污贿赂以提高国家的道德水平和管理**效率**。习近平认为贪污和贿赂不但会影响国家的经济和政治环境，也会大大地危害国家**形象**和社会公信力。

虽然《请投我一票》**记录**的是一群小学生选举班长的过程，但是影片中呈现的贪污和贿赂事件都**反映**着现实世界的问题。例如，成成贿赂不投他票的同学，并承诺如果自己当选就让他们担任学习委员、副班长等重要职位。

罗雷的父母在这次选举中 竭尽所能 地帮助罗雷赢得班长一职。他们先**邀请**罗雷的同班同学乘坐自己工作单位管理的轻轨。在投票前一天，罗雷的父亲更是**拿出**一沓粉色卡片，耳提面命 地告诉儿子，别忘了在投票前把卡片送给同学作为中秋节礼物。罗雷父母利用招待和送礼的方式使罗雷在这场选举中获得压倒性的胜利，**间接**地反映了在大人世界里，为了达到目的而 不择手段 的贿赂**现象**。

> 竭尽所能：用一切办法去完成任务或达成目标。
>
> 耳提面命：当面、恳切地提醒某人，多用于长辈对晚辈。
>
> 不择手段：为了达到目的，什么手段都使用，多指不正当的手段。

Activity 1 Put an X next to the correct statements. (There are four correct statements.)

A	习近平主席认为解决贪污和贿赂是一个重要的课题。
B	贪污是一种有利社会的行为。
C	贿赂是一种合法的行为。
D	如果没有贪污和贿赂，国家的管理效率可能会提高。
E	影片《请投我一票》没有反映目前的现实社会。
F	成成在学校霸凌不想投票给他的同学。
G	罗雷的父母没有帮助罗雷赢得班长选举。
H	给全班同学送中秋节卡片是罗雷父亲想出的一种贿赂手段。
I	影片《请投我一票》反映了现实世界中的贿赂现象。

Activity 2 Prepare a presentation on one of the following questions and deliver it to your class.

1 为什么习近平要重视打击贪污和贿赂？

2 贪污和贿赂会对一个国家的政治和经济带来什么负面影响？请举例说明。

3 贪污和贿赂会如何影响国家的形象和社会公信力？

4 在打击贪污和贿赂方面，中国政府还需要做出哪些努力？

Chapter

3

Summary and Scene Analysis

什么是民主?

大意

什么是民主? 什么是投票? 面对这两个问题,两位小朋友流露出疑惑的表情,一位**回答**"不知道",另外一位反复说着"投票"两个字。在升旗仪式上,罗雷担任执旗手,全校同学跟着晓菲高喊"爱国励志,自强不息!"五星红旗在风中冉冉升起,小朋友们开始唱国歌,好像作战的小士兵,一边踏着步,一边喊着相同的口号。升旗仪式过后,小朋友们在教学楼前拍完照,再各自回到教室上课。

Activity 1 Rewrite the sentence using the provided alternative phrases.

1 面对这两个问题,两位小朋友流露出疑惑的表情。

_____（对于　表现出　困惑的）

2 在升旗仪式上,罗雷担任执旗手。

_____（拿着国旗）

3 全校同学跟着晓菲高喊爱国口号。

_____（大声喊出）

4 五星红旗在风中冉冉升起。

_____（慢慢地升起）

For future revisions, simply choose the phrases that are easier for you to remember!

场景分析

在纪录片开头,导演用特写镜头**采访**了两位学生,让观众**近距离**地看到了小朋友疑惑的**面部**表情。观众也**直接**理解到影片中的小朋友其实并不清楚"民主"与"投票"的意思。

在升旗仪式的场景中，我们可以看到**天真**的孩童喊着爱国口号，表达着对国家的热爱，像作战的小士兵。通过升旗仪式前后的场景，我们发现小朋友在升旗仪式上**严肃**的样子与合影时的天真笑容**形成**了对比。此外，导演用 整齐划一 的队伍和小学生一起喊爱国口号的**画面**呈现了在西方学校少见的集体活动。

Activity **2** Complete the sentence by choosing the most suitable answer. Share alternative answers with the class.

1 在电影开头，导演用特写镜头采访两位学生，是为了 _____。

    A 娱乐观众   B 强调表情   C 展现他们的动作

    Alternative answer: _____

2 导演从旁观者的角度来拍摄是为了使观众 _____。

    A 置身事外   B 感受到导演的创意   C 身临其境

    Alternative answer: _____

3 在升旗仪式的场景中，我们没看到 _____。

    A 井然有序 的队伍   B 孩子们一起唱歌跳舞   C 小朋友踏着整齐的步伐

    Alternative answer: _____

4 小学生们戴着红领巾一起参加升旗仪式以及唱国歌的画面象征着 _____。

    A 团结和集体意识   B 对国家的信心   C 爱国精神

    Alternative answer: _____

Activity **3** Fill the gap using 的, 得 or 地.

> **Challenge**
>
> These sentences are polished with more advanced phrases. Learn those highlighted phrases to make your sentences more complex and sophisticated!

1 两位 天真无邪 _____ 小朋友流露出疑惑的表情。

2 五星红旗 缓缓 _____ 升起。

3 大家在操场上 朝气蓬勃 _____ 唱着国歌。

4 我们可以看到 相同年龄 _____ 孩子们 反复 _____ 喊着相同的口号。

5 原本活泼好动的孩子 整整齐齐 _____ 喊着"前进！前进！前进！"

6 小朋友们在 井然有序 _____ 队伍中做着一样的事并喊着爱国口号。

7 升旗仪式过后，小朋友们在教学楼前 高兴 _____ 拍照，再各自回到教室上课。

8 小学生们在操场上站 _____ 整整齐齐，一起高喊着爱国口号。

三位候选人

01:28—03:16

大意

　　新的学期，新的希望，新的**要求**！班主任张老师一上课就向大家**宣布**这学期要开展民主选举班长的活动，同学们都感到新鲜和好奇。学校老师提名了三位候选人，分别是罗雷、成成和许晓菲。三位候选人被班主任请到台上，听着班主任对民主投票的解释。

　　那么投票的方式是什么样的呢？老师清楚地告诉每一位同学他们都有**发表**自己意见的权利，可以选择自己喜欢、信任的候选人，把自己手中的选票投给他／她。最后得票最多的候选人将成为这学期的班长，这就是民主投票。老师也提到：在选举的过程中，候选人可以选择一到两名同学，作为他／她的竞选小帮手。

　　放学时间到了，伴随着爱国主义歌曲，班主任把学生带到教室外，这时候家长已在校外等着接自己的孩子回家。

Activity 1 Write the name of the following characters.

Activity 2 Rewrite 被 sentence using 把 structure.

例如
"诚实勇敢"四个字**被**学校挂在每间教室的墙上。
▶ 学校**把**"诚实勇敢"四个字挂在每间教室的墙上。

1 三位候选人被老师请到台上。
_____

2 学生被老师带到教室外。
_____

3 孩子被家长接回家。
_____

4 "民主"二字被老师写在黑板上。
_____

5 "民主"的意思被老师解释清楚了吗?
_____

Activity 3 Look up the following expressions and fill in the appropriate phrase in the blank.

A 陆陆续续　　　B 诚实勇敢　　　C 好学多思
D 心不在焉　　　E 一字排开　　　F 身临其境

1 升旗仪式后,小朋友 _____ 进入了教室。

2 当班主任讲解班长选举规则时,导演使用交错的镜头让观众看到小朋友们似乎有点儿 _____。

3 三位候选人在台上 _____。

4 导演也用了窗外旁观者的视角让观众 _____。

5 导演用中景呈现黑板上的"民主"二字与墙上的"_____、_____"。

(Extension) 找出上面句子的相关镜头。

🏫 场景分析

　　升旗仪式后，小朋友 陆陆续续 进入教室。这时导演运用近景镜头介绍张老师，也就是三位候选人的班主任。在电影的开头，导演也用了几个近景镜头来暗示影片中的三位中心**人物**（成成、许晓菲和罗雷）。

　　当班主任在讲解班长选举规则时，导演使用老师和学生交错的镜头让观众看到班上的学生似乎有点儿 心不在焉 ，以及对选举规则的陌生。导演还用窗外旁观者的**视角**让观众 身临其境 ，并能观察到教室内的**状况**。

　　三位候选人在台上 一字排开 时，导演用全景镜头呈现黑板上的"民主"二字与墙上的"诚实勇敢 、好学多思"，**传达**了民主选举需要具备的素质。放学的时候，背景中的爱国歌曲唱出"我们是共产主义接班人"，再次表达了国家对小学生们的期望。

Activity 4 Draw the positions of human figures 🧍 according to types of camera shots and select the function of each shot from the options below.

远景	全景	中景
作用：		
近景	特写	
作用：		

A　通常用来表现人物之间的关系以及感情的交流。

B　可以近距离地观察人物的表情和情绪。

C　表现人物在环境中的全身动作。

D　通常用来介绍或展现影片中的环境。

E　细节地展现人物的心情、内心世界或面部表情，更接近观众。

三位候选人与他们的家庭

03:17—07:17

大意

　　三位候选人分别回到家。对于孩子参与班长选举，家长们似乎都十分支持。成成想当班长是因为他认为当上班长就能拥有很大的权利，同学们都会对他 言听计从 。班长要求同学站，所有人都得站；要求大家坐，大家都得坐。成成的**继父**教导他：民主是人民当家作主。罗雷回到家后，父母主动询问是否要帮他准备班长选举，罗雷肯定地告诉父母，他想靠自己的**实力**，不想**控制**别人。相较于成成与罗雷，晓菲显得比较害羞，不想说话，只听妈妈说。夜深了，小候选人们却已经 紧锣密鼓 地开始**练习**才艺表演。

Activity 1 Who made the following statement 成成, 罗雷 or 晓菲?

1 要靠自己真正的实力。＿＿＿＿＿＿

2 我要说什么？＿＿＿＿＿＿

3 老爸，"民主"到底是什么意思？＿＿＿＿＿＿

4 留一点儿时间让我看一会儿电视。＿＿＿＿＿＿

5 不要控制别人，让他们自己想。＿＿＿＿＿＿

6 班长有权利，让同学坐下同学就得坐下。＿＿＿＿＿＿

(Extension) 讨论他们为什么说这些话。

Activity 2 Do all three candidates react the same way when they find out they are nominated for class monitor? Watch this section of the film and take notes based on the following questions.

1 他们各自表现出什么样的态度？说了什么？

2 他们了解民主选举的意义吗？为什么？

成成: _____

_____

_____

罗雷: _____

_____

_____

晓菲: _____

_____

_____

Now, make a presentation on your notes to your class. You may start with...

回到家后，三位候选人分别有不同的态度及表现。

首先，我们可以看到成成……；再来是罗雷，……；最后晓菲……

从他 / 她说的话，我们可以理解……

从他 / 她的言行 / 态度，我们发现 / 观察到……

他 / 她表现出……

就……来看，她 / 他并不了解……

场景分析

　　镜头转到三位候选人的家里，导演在这一段用蒙太奇（montage）的剪辑手法分别呈现了三位候选人的性格**差异**，以及不同的家庭教养方式。为了增加真实感，贴近观众的感受，导演走进候选人家中拍摄，大多时候**运用**近景与中景跟拍的方式来记录三位候选人与家长的互动和**对话**。

首先，站在旁观者的角度，我们观察到成成仍然不**理解**民主的意思。从学校回到家后，他再一次询问继父：民主到底是什么意思？其他的画面，如妈妈的宠爱以及成成对妈妈的不耐烦，使观众感觉到成成像是个"小皇帝"。

在下一段画面中，我们可以看到罗雷家门前有一辆汽车。客厅里的大鱼缸也说明罗雷父母有较高的社会经济地位。罗雷的性格在他和父母的对话中 一览无遗 ，当罗雷说出"靠实力，不要控制别人"时，导演特地**采用**特写镜头让观众看到罗雷的坚定和作为现任班长的自信。尽管**拒绝**了父母的帮助，罗雷的妈妈仍然干涉起罗雷的长笛练习。即使导演利用中景镜头，观众仍能清楚地看到罗雷在昏暗的小房间内无助的面部表情，说明此刻他也开始感受到妈妈给他的压力。

然而与前两位候选人**相比**，晓菲的态度更加**平淡**温和。通过近距离观察晓菲和妈妈在床边的对话，我们感受到晓菲的安静。不想说话或许是因为对选举没信心。晓菲的妈妈耐心地引导她积极地参与班长竞选，说出自己的想法，加深大家对她的**印象**，让大家了解并支持她。

Activity 3 Based on the analysis above, jot down 3 or 4 key points and describe their impacts, symbolic meanings, metaphors, or reasons in your own words. An example is provided.

重点一

Eg: 导演使用蒙太奇手法分别呈现了三位候选人回到家后不同的表现，以及他们与家人互动的方式，使观众更能理解三位小朋友性格上的差异。

重点二

重点三

☆ **重点四**

"打倒晓菲"事件

07:18—11:50

大意

　　教室中，伴随着助选小**伙伴**的舞蹈，晓菲用长笛吹出了《梁祝》的**旋律**。她们一会儿要一起上台，向同学们**展示**练习的成果。上台前，晓菲妈妈陪伴晓菲一句句地练习演讲。

　　然而，这个时候，成成正偷偷地在教室外面观察。当他看到晓菲的才艺表演似乎 略胜一筹 时，成成的心中生出了一个坏**想法**：他想联合同学们一起打倒晓菲。于是在才艺表演前，成成要求他的助选小伙伴在晓菲表演时**起哄**，说晓菲表演得不好。

　　才艺表演刚刚开始，晓菲在台上显得 手足无措 。听同学们喊着"打倒晓菲"，晓菲**哭**了。老师**只好**先把晓菲带到教室外休息，然后严肃地告诉大家，不可以用这样的方式来攻击候选人，要以文明、友善的方式**欣赏**候选人的演讲与表演。后来，成成也到教室外跟晓菲 赔不是 。

　　晓菲**整理**好情绪后又回到了台上，她**接受**了成成和其他同学的道歉，强忍着情绪和泪水**完成**了自己的才艺表演。

> **The cultural highlight**
> Research the story of
> liáng shān bó yǔ zhù yīng tái
> 梁 山 伯 与 祝 英 台

Activity 1 Replace advanced expressions in the highlighted sections using the ones provided.

Ⓐ 紧张　　Ⓑ 更优秀　　Ⓒ 道歉　　Ⓓ 说悄悄话　　Ⓔ 好像在思考

1 成成看到晓菲的才艺表演似乎 略胜一筹 。＿＿＿＿＿＿

2 晓菲在台上显得 手足无措 。＿＿＿＿＿＿

3 成成也到教室外跟晓菲 赔不是 。＿＿＿＿＿＿

4 我们能观察到成成 若有所思 。＿＿＿＿＿＿

5 导演利用近景镜头强调同学们 交头接耳 的表情及对话。＿＿＿＿＿＿

Activity 2   Find the English meanings of the following emotion words.

正面的情绪		负面的情绪	
中文	英文	中文	英文
yú kuài 愉快		jǔ sàng yù mèn 沮丧 / 郁闷	
dàn rán 淡然		shī wàng 失望	
kāi xīn 开心		wú lì 无力	
zì xìn 自信		nán guò shāng gǎn xīn suān 难过 / 伤感 / 心酸	
lè guān 乐观		bèi mào fàn qì fèn 被冒犯 / 气愤	
huó pō 活泼		cuò zhé cuò bài 挫折 / 挫败	
xīng fèn xǐ yuè 兴奋 / 喜悦		bèi gū lì 被孤立	
sōng yì kǒu qì 松一口气		dà shòu dǎ jī 大受打击	

Activity 3   Describe how Xiaofei's emotions changed over the course of the talent show using the following structures and suitable phrases.

(Extension)   解释为什么她会有那样的情绪。

晓菲的表情 / 态度 / 行为透露出……   晓菲表现出……   晓菲显得……

晓菲的脸上**写着**……   晓菲感到 / 觉得……

Eg 1   才艺表演开始前，晓菲表现出积极的态度，一直练习吹长笛，因为她想赢得班长选举。

Eg 2   才艺表演开始前，晓菲在卫生间里开始感到不自信，她问妈妈如果说错了怎么办。

1   第一次上台时……

2   第二次上台时……

3   才艺表演结束时……

Activity 4 Discussion.

1 晓菲和妈妈在做什么？

2 导演使用了什么镜头？

3 成成和小伙伴交头接耳，小声说了什么？

4 晓菲为什么哭了？

5 成成为什么向晓菲道歉？

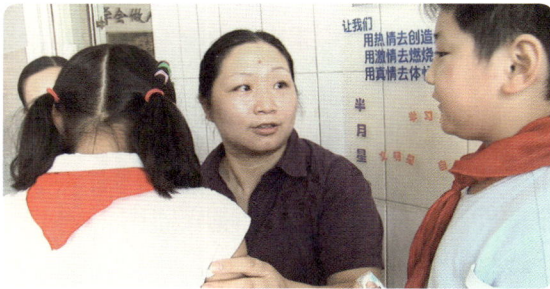

6 导演以什么镜头访问晓菲妈妈？晓菲妈妈说了什么？

场景分析

Activity 5 Circle the appropriate answer to complete the analysis.

在晓菲才艺表演的场景中，导演运用了一些摄影技巧记录"打倒晓菲"事件，详细地展现了成成和晓菲的性格以及同学们之间的**冲突**。

在晓菲才艺表演前，我们首先看到镜头中呈现了两位小伙伴的舞蹈／歌唱／戏剧，完美地配合了晓菲的钢琴／长笛／吉他表演，表现出晓菲对才艺秀／辩论／演讲的充分准备及重视。她想告诉大家，她会是一位"好学、能干、能给大家带来难过／快乐的班长"。对于这一段的画面，导演大多使用了中景镜头／特写镜头，使观众清楚地看到晓菲**母女**以及晓菲和小伙伴们的**交流**互动。

与此同时，成成正在窗外看着晓菲的才艺练习。通过中景镜头／跟拍镜头，我们能观察到成成 若有所思 。之后，成成要求他的老师／父母／小伙伴在晓菲表演的时候起哄 ／ 大哭 ／ 说话，导演利用了中景／近景镜头强调他们 交头接耳 的表情以及秘密的对话。

才艺表演中，我们看到许多对比及冲突／和平的画面。冲突的**场面**使得站在台上的晓菲开始感到生气／紧张。例如，我们看到**一群**同学说着"晓菲最棒"，另外一群同学则大声喊着"打倒晓菲"，二者形成对比。晓菲的无力感与同学们的吵闹声，骂人／大笑／**哭泣**的女同学与哭泣／唱歌／闹事的男同学都形成了对比。

事件之后，成成先向晓菲道歉。"我代表罗雷向你道歉"，成成小声地跟晓菲说。导演也通过特写镜头／中景镜头强调了成成**矛盾／满足／**后悔的表情。之后成成再让罗雷向晓菲赔不是／**开玩笑／**说悄悄话。这里我们看到成成态度的 180 度大**转变**，从"打倒晓菲"事件的计划者转变成**爱护**、支持晓菲的好同学。

才艺表演结束后，导演用全身镜头／特写镜头／近景镜头来拍摄晓菲妈妈的采访。采访中，她认为晓菲**缺乏**自信主要是因为晓菲来自单亲家庭。晓菲妈妈兴奋／难过地说："我没有给她一个很好的家。"通过晓菲妈妈的采访，我们更能了解晓菲的**成长**背景／愿望／考试成绩。

成成的才艺秀

大意

　　在上一位候选人晓菲的才艺表演结束后，**接着**上台的是成成。成成的才艺是**演唱**一首拿手的**流行**歌曲。在才艺秀前，他带着两位小伙伴到**空**教室练习，他的小伙伴还给他提了意见。

　　表演时，成成 胸有成竹 地带着小伙伴一起上台。演唱的过程中，他表现得十分自信，在台上他还和台下的同学互动，教室里的**气氛**非常**热闹**，像是一个**小型演唱会**。逐渐被气氛**感染**的同学们渐渐地开始大声地说支持成成。当场面渐渐失去控制时，成成大叫了一声"安静！"全班都安静下来了。

　　成成走下台，许多同学跟他握手**表示**支持。放学回家后，成成跟爸爸妈妈说自己的才艺秀很成功，他似乎有当上了班长的感觉，感到相当开心，还想再尝试一次。

> **The cultural highlight**
> gū dān běi bàn qiú
> 孤单北半球 is the song sung by 成成. Find the full version of the song and enjoy it!

Activity 1 **Select the alternative explanation for the highlighted section.**

Ⓐ 非常有自信　　Ⓑ 好像在现场　　Ⓒ 问答　　Ⓓ 积极地把事情做好

1 成成 胸有成竹 地带着小伙伴一起上台。＿＿＿＿＿＿

2 观众可以感受到成成 求好心切 的态度和自信。＿＿＿＿＿

3 成成用 一问一答 的方式使全班同学更投入。＿＿＿＿＿

4 导演从不同的角度拍摄，使观众 身临其境 。＿＿＿＿＿

Activity 2 Discussion.

1 导演使用了什么镜头？

2 为什么成成的小伙伴拥抱成成？

3 成成怎么向台下的同学拉票？

4 成成为什么看起来很开心？

场景分析

Activity 3 Complete the following sentences using the phrases provided.

(Extension) 找出对应的场景。

> A 流行　　 B 如何　　 C 中心　　 D 练习　　 E 记录　　 F 接着　　 G 各种

_____ 晓菲表演的是成成的才艺秀。导演大多时候使用中景和半身镜头来_____ 成成（**候选人**）和同学们（**选民**）成功的互动和_____选举手段。

在才艺秀之前，观众可以感受到成成的 求好心切 。导演用了**全景**镜头来拍摄成成的画面。成成站在画面的_____点，用妈妈教他的唱歌技巧唱出自己准备的歌曲。同时，成成也和小伙伴们讨论_____让他的表演更完美。

A 中心人物	**B** 镜头	**C** 利用	**D** 支持	**E** 提高

在才艺秀的过程中，我们可以看到成成利用了**宣传**、口号、承诺和拉票等选举手段来 _____ 同学们对自己的支持度。

在宣传方面，成成唱歌时，他安排两位小伙伴分别上台和自己拥抱，并站在他身后 _____ 他。导演 _____ 中景镜头拍摄，成成继续作为 _____ 站在镜头的中间，像个偶像**明星**在开**个人**演唱会。_____ 转到班上的同学，我们可以看到同学们**投入**的表情，他们**拍着手**和成成一起唱歌，大家似乎都十分欣赏他的表演。

A 从	**B** 互动	**C** 角度	**D** 表演	**E** 旁观者	**F** 看起来	**G** 方式

在口号方面，成成唱完歌后，右边的小伙伴问大家："他唱得好不好？"成成也问："大家支不支持我？"成成和小伙伴用 一问一答 的 _____ 带动了班上的气氛，使全班同学更投入了。导演以 _____ 的 _____ 拍摄，使我们像是在才艺表演的现场，同时 _____ 后面的**角度**来拍摄，使观众能看到全班同学的**注意**力都集中在台上的成成身上。

在承诺方面，搭配着请求的手势，成成说："投我一票，我再给你们 _____ 更好的**节目**，要不要？"镜头里的画面 _____ 像是真实的候选人与选民的 _____，**折射**出成人世界的选举**文化**。

A 联想到	**B** 拥有	**C** 通过	**D** 关系	**E** 拍摄	**F** 展现	**G** 导演

在拉票环节，_____ 用跟拍的方式 _____ 成成 _____ 拥抱、握手、说方言和有趣的口音来拉票，并称呼同学们"兄弟"和"大妹子"以拉近他和同学们的 _____。

同时，成成也用了他班长候选人的身份 _____ 他的权利。例如，他大声地喊出"安静！"来维持班级秩序，**令**我们 _____ 成成说过当班长就会 _____ 最大的权利，同学们都必须服从他的命令。

Activity 4

Discuss the following questions about Cheng Cheng's talent show and fill in the table.

成成的才艺表演	他做了／说了什么？	什么样的镜头和画面？
手段一 _____		
手段二 _____		
手段三 _____		
手段四 _____		

现任班长的忧虑

大意

才艺表演的第二天，音乐课下课后，成成找到晓菲，要她为昨天**发生**的"打倒晓菲"事件报复罗雷。晓菲很**善良**，不敢答应，拒绝了成成。然而成成又找了其他同学在罗雷表演时 起哄 。

罗雷表演时，成成偷偷地跟老师说，妈妈教了他一些 招数 。表演完后，成成跟一群同学**批评**罗雷打人和威胁别人的**言行**，罗雷**看起来**受到了打击。

午饭时，一位排队拿饭的同学表示罗雷总是打人，因此不会支持他。罗雷听到同学说他坏话，感到难堪，马上 反击 。其他同学也表达了自己的意见及支持的候选人，也有人不知道要选谁。罗雷和成成也互相问了对方怎么投票。

罗雷自己也问了一些同学要投票给谁，或许是同学的**反应**使罗雷感到**忧虑**，于是他跟一位同学说想**放弃**竞选班长，那位同学也马上跟成成说了罗雷想放弃的想法。成成听到后开心极了，也更积极地通过 利诱 的方式让同学投票给他。

> **The cultural highlights**
>
> The song that Luo Lei sang at his talent show is called 童 话 tóng huà. The singer of this song is 光 良 guāng liáng from Malaysia.

Activity 1 **Answer the following questions based on the film and learn how to use the key phrases.**

1 同学们和成成是怎么对罗雷的表演 起哄 的？

_____

A 句子中"起哄"的词性是什么？（动词 / 名词 / 形容词）
B 哪一个词可以替换"起哄"？（大声说话 / 捣乱 / 开玩笑）
C "起哄声"的意思是什么？

2 罗雷才艺表演的时候，成成用什么样的 招数 打击罗雷？

_____

A 句子中"招数"的词性是什么？（动词 / 名词 / 形容词）

B 哪个词不能替换"招数"？（策略 / 手段 / 办法）

3 成成是怎么 利诱 同学的？他跟同学说了什么？

_____

A 句子中"利诱"的词性是什么？（名词 / 动词 / 形容词）

B "利诱"的意思是什么？（用……来引诱）

C "副班长"和"学习委员"的意思是什么？

4 午饭排队时罗雷听到同学说他坏话，他是怎么向那位同学 反击 的？他说了什么？

_____

A 句子中"反击"的词性是什么？（名词 / 动词 / 形容词）

B 哪一个词不能替换"反击"？（回击 / 还击 / 打击）

Activity **2** Read the following sentences and put them in the correct order according to the film.

A 成成表示愿意投票给罗雷。   B 成成跟老师说妈妈教他的打击罗雷的招数。

C 罗雷说想退出班长选举。   D 成成在教室后面起哄，说罗雷唱歌唱得不好。

E 成成让晓菲报复罗雷。   F 成成用副班长的职位利诱同学给他投票。

G 午饭时罗雷听到同学说他坏话。

Activity **3** Discussion.

1 罗雷准备了什么表演？   **2** 成成和老师说了什么？

3 成成联合同学对罗雷做了什么？

4 罗雷对同学小声说了什么？

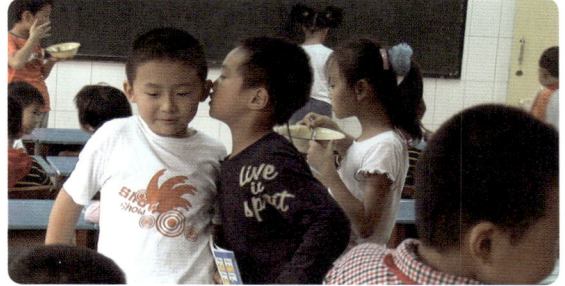

5 成成用什么来利诱同学？

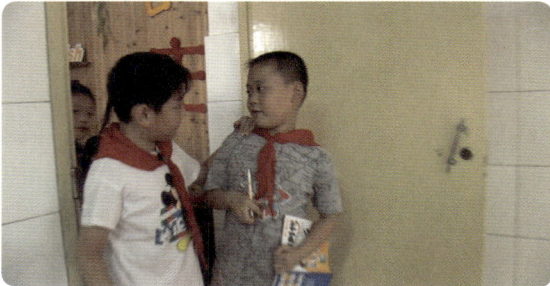

6 成成对晓菲说了什么？导演用了什么样的镜头？

Activity 4 Use the following structure and phrases to describe unkind behaviour you observe in the film.

霸凌者	联合 伙同 说服 跟 / 和 要	同学 另外一位候选人 小伙伴 晓菲 罗雷	来	攻击 / 打击 / 打倒 报复 欺负 / 欺凌 霸凌 责骂 / 骂 批评 / 批判 威胁	被霸凌者 受害者
				起哄。 捣乱。	

_____

_____

_____

_____

_____

场景分析

Activity 5 Circle the appropriate answer to complete the analysis.

首先，我们看到美丽的校园，操场上玩耍的学童，和在音乐课上**认真**合唱的小朋友们。导演用远景 / 中景 / 近景特别拍摄了在唱歌 / 跳舞 / 玩耍的罗雷，也就是今天才艺表演的**主角 / 配角** / 导演。导演使用一些画面，例如**校园**的场景、玩耍的学童和上课的小朋友**提醒**我们三位候选人仍然是成熟 / **厉害** / 天真的学童，是学校的一分子。

下一个画面中，我们可以看到成成与晓菲在讲悄悄话。原来，成成希望晓菲**打扰** / 报复 / 放弃罗雷。导演利用半身镜头 / 全身镜头 / 全景镜头从成成的身后拍摄，让我们能清楚看到晓菲担心的表情，以及晓菲回答成成"我不敢"。成成的行为与晓菲的反应体现了两人性格上的不同。

为了今天的才艺秀，罗雷准备了长笛和唱歌表演。而**另外**两位候选人只准备了一项才艺，可以看出罗雷表现出了作为现任 / 前任班长的好胜心。表演开始时，导演移动镜头 / 照相机 / 照片让我们看到班上同学期待的表情，我们也看到成成和老师 交头接耳，他跟老师说："等罗雷唱歌时，要说他唱得不好！"老师微笑地反问："你妈妈教你的？"老师与成成的对话令我们 恍然大悟 （ ＝**突然明白** ） 原来家长已经开始介入这场班长选举。

罗雷唱歌时，导演使用近景 / 远景 / 中景拍摄成成批评罗雷、叫罗雷下台时的面部表情。表演结束后，成成联合其他同学一起叫着"罗雷！罗雷！威胁别人！"等口号。"打倒晓菲"事件似乎又再次**出现**，事件的主人公却换成了罗雷。

　　午饭的时候，导演使用和同学<u>近距离访谈</u> / 远距离访谈的方式来了解**各**候选人的支持度，镜头刚好拍到罗雷正在<u>支持</u> / 威胁 / 鼓励一位受访者，这位受访者说起罗雷总是打人。我们可以看到罗雷生气地对受访同学说，"像你这样的孩子，我必须严格，不严格你就不会听我的。"展现了罗雷当班长时管理班级的方式。之后导演也拍到了成成和罗雷的对话，成成对罗雷说："我跟妈妈说想投票给你，因为我喜欢你。"成成似乎想利用心理战使罗雷**相信**成成会把票投给他。

　　投票前的考试 / <u>调查</u> / 选举结果令成成十分满意。导演利用罗雷自信 / **失望** / **感动**的画面对比成成开心得意的画面，令观众相信成成会赢得这场班长选举。

Activity 6 Discuss the following questions regarding talent shows and record your answers in Chinese

	晓菲	成成	罗雷
表演了什么才艺？			
他 / 她的家长是怎么帮助他们练习才艺表演的？			
他们是怎么对其他候选人起哄的？			
被欺负的时候他们有什么反应？			

罗雷父母献计
——轻轨之旅

18:15—21:11

大意

在警察局工作的爸爸**建议**罗雷邀请同学们一起去坐轻轨。这样一方面可以带同学看看最新、最**现代化**的交通工具，另一方面也可以**借**这次机会和同学们多交流，增进**感情**和**友谊**。**本来**想靠自己实力赢得班长选举的罗雷，最后点头接受了爸妈的提议。

校外教学当天，罗雷的父母先在轻轨**月台**帮孩子们照相，为大家留下美好的**回忆**。拍照时，小朋友们大喊"茄子！"每个人看起来都非常**愉快**。在轻轨上，罗雷父母向孩子们介绍轻轨**设施**，以及轻轨外的城市风景。罗雷也向同学展现了自己的**热情**，在小巴士上唱歌带动气氛。成成看到同学们和罗雷一路上有说有笑， 心中不是滋味 。

快乐出游的一天结束了，罗雷吹着口哨回家并跟妈妈说之前不想给他投票的同学现在也想投给他了。妈妈觉得罗雷 打铁要趁热 ，应该问问大家喜不喜欢这次轻轨之旅，要不要把选票投给他，但是罗雷不想再继续听从妈妈给他的意见。

回到学校后，成成觉得自己的选票已经被罗雷**拉**走了，向老师表达了放弃的想法，老师鼓励他回家后和爸爸妈妈谈谈。然而回到家后，妈妈以胡锦涛作为例子要成成不能放弃班长选举。

> **The cultural highlight**
>
> Whi e it's common for Westerners to say the word "cheese" when taking photos, in China, the term
> qié zi
> "茄子" meaning "aubergine", is frequently used.

Activity 1 Select the alternative explanation for the highlighted section.

Ⓐ 内心感到不好受 Ⓑ 提供计策 Ⓒ 用尽全力 Ⓓ 一句话都不说 Ⓔ 把握时机

1 罗雷父母 献计 。_____

2 妈妈觉得罗雷 打铁要趁热 。_____

3 罗雷父母为了帮罗雷赢得班长选举 全力以赴 。_____

4 成成看到同学们和罗雷玩得开心， 心中不是滋味 ，在公车上 一言不发 。＿＿＿＿＿＿
＿＿＿＿＿

Activity 2 **Read the sentences below. Decide whether the underlined word is a verb, noun, or adjective.**

中文词性

动词

名词

形容词

1 罗雷父母<u>献</u>计。＿＿＿＿＿＿＿＿＿＿

2 导演从成成的背后给了小伙伴<u>生气</u>的面部表情<u>特写</u>。
＿＿＿＿＿＿＿＿＿

3 导演运用中景和特写镜头来<u>拍摄</u>罗雷的**身体**语言和面部表情。＿＿＿＿＿＿＿＿＿＿

4 真实的画面让角色的<u>呈现</u>更<u>深刻</u>。＿＿＿＿＿＿＿＿

5 通过<u>真实</u>画面的<u>传达</u>，观众看到三位候选人都呈现出自信与不自信的一面。＿＿＿＿＿＿
＿＿＿＿

6 他们忙着拍照，<u>娱乐</u>罗雷的同学们，<u>凸显</u>出他们为了让罗雷赢得班长选举 尽心尽力 。
＿＿＿＿＿＿＿＿＿

7 成成脸上的<u>表情</u>逐渐<u>变得</u>严肃。＿＿＿＿＿＿＿＿

8 导演特地<u>拉近</u>镜头拍摄成成烦恼的表情。＿＿＿＿＿＿＿

9 轻轨之旅后，成成开始因为罗雷比他更<u>受欢迎</u>而烦恼。＿＿＿＿＿＿＿＿＿

(**Extension**) 讨论上面哪些词语有一个以上的词性。

场景分析

　　罗雷想要放弃的想法被他父母知道了，于是他们建议带全班同学坐轻轨，这也是改变选举结果的**转折点**。

　　首先，罗雷反问父母为什么要邀请同学坐轻轨，父母耐心地解释轻轨之旅会给罗雷带来什么样的优势，要罗雷坐轻轨的时候跟同学们增加感情和友谊。导演运用中景和特写镜头的交错来拍摄罗雷的身体语言和面部表情。罗雷在思考父母建议时，我们可以从他的反应和肢体语言中看出他的犹豫以及挣扎的**心情**。

　　在下一个画面中，我们看到一栋蓝色的**建筑物**。罗雷手**拿**喇叭带领大家走上轻轨月台。手拿喇叭象征着今天他是领导，他有说话的权利。其次，我们看到罗雷的父母全程主导这次的校外教学。他们忙着拍照，**取悦**罗雷的同学们，这里表现出他们为了帮助罗雷赢得班长选举 全力以赴 。

在轻轨上，成成似乎跟其他同学起了**争执**，其中一位是成成的**亲密**小伙伴。导演从成成的背后给了小伙伴生气的面部表情**特写**，使我们感觉到他开始对成成的言行感到不满。对比其他孩子的愉快气氛，成成的表情逐渐**变得**严肃。听到同学们在巴士上唱着罗雷才艺表演的歌曲，成成 一言不发 ，此时导演也特地拉近镜头拍摄了成成**烦恼**的表情。

轻轨之旅以后，成成向妈妈和老师表示想放弃班长选举。然而妈妈跟成成说："不能退出！这才第一步，你还要**当**胡锦涛呢！"妈妈拿胡锦涛作为例子鼓励成成，因为对成成来说，成为像胡锦涛那样有权力的领导是成功的象征。

通过这些真实的镜头画面，我们看到三位候选人呈现出自信与不自信的一面，这些让角色的呈现更深刻，也使观众对接下来的**情节**发展更感兴趣。

Activity 3 Based on the analysis above, jot down 3 or 4 key points and describe their impacts, symbolic meanings, metaphors, or reasons in your own words.

重点一

重点二

重点三

☆ 重点四

Activity 4 Discuss the symbolic meanings of the underlined objects.

人：

1 影片中妈妈提到成成想成为<u>胡锦涛那样的人</u>，成为像胡锦涛一样的人物象征着 _____
_____。

"象征"的意思是用具体的人事物来传达某种意义。

事：

2 小学生在学校<u>唱爱国歌曲</u>、<u>戴红领巾</u>象征着 <u>   </u> 。

3 对成成来说，<u>选上班长</u>象征着 <u>   </u> 。

物：

4 影片中，上月台的<u>电扶梯</u>和<u>轻轨</u>是<u>城市现代化</u>的象征。

5 罗雷在电扶梯上拿着喇叭，走在队伍前的画面象征着 <u>   </u> 。

6 罗雷家的<u>大鱼缸</u>和<u>大房子</u>象征着 <u>   </u> 。

(**Extension**) 想想其他有象征意义的场景

成成与晓菲的辩论赛

21:12—27:20

大意

　　辩论赛将在几天后开始。首先上场辩论的是晓菲和成成。晓菲的**母亲**了解晓菲的性格，面对即将**到来**的辩论赛，她给了晓菲很多建议，例如，"要 以理服人 ""不要害怕""要去**尝试**"。妈妈跟晓菲做了一些辩论练习，**并且**教她如何回应别人的问题，她还建议晓菲找两位小伙伴收集其他候选人的缺点。

　　到学校后，三位候选人积极地**访问**同学。成成认为晓菲的缺点没有罗雷多，成成妈妈看到成成 重拾信心 ，于是继续鼓励他。

　　辩论的时候，成成和晓菲相互指出对方的缺点。同时，成成还说当班长应该 以身作则 ，必须起到带头**作用**。最后，其他同学也开始加入辩论，罗雷也站起来批评成成，指出他 不好的地方 。下课后成成生气地**找**罗雷理论，两人争执起来。成成批评罗雷" 不切实际"，罗雷说成成"没有真正的实力！"旁边的女同学也表现出对成成的不满。接着，成成又去找晓菲**谈话**，但晓菲不想理他，晓菲跟其他女同学都觉得成成 爱出风头 ，还有很强的 好胜 心。

| Activity | 1 | Select the alternative explanation for the highlighted section. |

> Ⓐ 用道理令人信服　Ⓑ 太爱表现自己　Ⓒ 以自己作为榜样　Ⓓ 不实际
> Ⓔ 缺点　Ⓕ 再次有了信心　Ⓖ 处处赢过别人　Ⓗ 快要到来
> Ⓘ 完全呈现　Ⓙ 说一套，做一套

1 晓菲的妈妈要晓菲 以理服人 。＿＿＿＿＿＿

2 成成妈妈非常高兴成成能 重拾信心 。＿＿＿＿＿＿

3 成成说当班长应该 以身作则 ，必须起到带头作用。＿＿＿＿＿＿

4 罗雷也站起来批评成成，指出他 不好的地方 。＿＿＿＿＿＿

5 成成骂罗雷 "不切实际"。_____

6 晓菲跟其他女同学觉得成成 爱出风头 ，还有很强的 好胜 心。_____

7 晓菲的妈妈告诉晓菲应该如何准备 即将到来 的辩论赛。_____

8 成成的真实性格在辩论后 一览无遗 。_____

9 成成的 言行不一 。_____

Activity 2 Who do the following weaknesses apply to?

- Ⓐ 爱哭
- Ⓑ 打人
- Ⓒ 上课和同学说话
- Ⓓ 作业没做完
- Ⓔ 话太多
- Ⓕ 爱自作主张
- Ⓖ 吃饭吃得慢
- Ⓗ 下课玩得疯
- Ⓘ 爱出风头
- Ⓙ 好胜

_____

_____

_____

场景分析

　　辩论比赛前，晓菲和妈妈在游乐园游玩的画面缓和了成成和妈妈对话带来的紧张感。与成成烦恼的表情相比，晓菲在游乐园的表情似乎显得更为**轻松**。两个画面对比，暗示着父母的期望影响着孩子，高期望会给孩子带来更多的压力。

导演**从**各个角度来拍摄、记录晓菲和妈妈在游乐园的对话与互动。从两人的肢体语言我们可以看出，晓菲母女俩的关系非常亲密，这**显示**出晓菲对妈妈的依赖。妈妈对晓菲应该如何准备 即将到来 的辩论赛给出了建议，她希望晓菲说话、做事都要有计划。"以理服人"是晓菲妈妈认为最重要的价值观。

相比之下，成成比晓菲更清楚应该怎么准备即将到来的辩论赛。吃饭的时候，成成自信地跟父母说他为辩论所做的准备，导演使用特写镜头来拍摄成成自信满满的表情。妈妈夸奖成成道："你是知道怎么去竞争的。"由此可见，成成的妈妈鼓励成成在竞争中勇于**争取**。

两人辩论时，晓菲以一种冷静客观的**语气**说出成成的缺点。等晓菲说完后，成成马上以一种严厉的语气说起晓菲的缺点，并要晓菲为她的缺点做出解释。辩论过程中，导演将拍摄视角移到了观看辩论比赛的同学们，令观众更有参与感。

成成的真实性格在辩论赛后 一览无遗 。下课后，他生气地去找罗雷理论。在争执中，成成说了脏话，还责怪罗雷之前批评他，跟教室后面黑板上写的"文明有礼""规范行为"的口号形成强烈的对比，好像在暗示成成的 言行不一 。

在影片中还出现了一些对比画面，例如，美好平静的校园与教室内因**各种**选举**活动产生**纷争的场景形成了对比。此外，我们还能看到学校集体活动与个人行为的差异。例如，全校学生一起跳课间操，参加升旗仪式，一起朗读。这些都暗示着身为学校的一员，三位候选人除了追求成为班长的个人荣誉，他们在学校也有应该承担的责任和义务。学校不仅是学生学习知识的地方，更是培养他们团队精神，让他们**共同**学习成长的地方。

Activity 3 Rewrite the following sentences using the provided structures, which are used to describe a distinct contrast or juxtaposition.

Ⓐ A 和 B 产生对比　　Ⓑ A 和 B 形成鲜明的对比　　Ⓒ A 和 B 呈现了明显的反差

1 与成成烦恼的表情相比，晓菲在游乐园的表情似乎显得更为轻松。

2 晓菲以一种非批判的语气说完成成的缺点。等晓菲说完后，成成马上以一种严厉的语气说起晓菲的缺点。

3 在争执中，成成朝着罗雷骂脏话，还责怪罗雷批评他，跟教室后面黑板上的"文明有礼""规范行为"的标语形成强烈的对比。

4 导演还对比呈现了校园和教室中的场景，用校园里平静的画面与教室里辩论的冲突形成对比。

---

5 影片中常常出现用学校集体活动和个人竞选活动做比较的场景。

(Extension) 找出其他对比画面的例子并解释其含义。

罗雷与成成的辩论赛

27:21—35:08

大意

　　放学后，罗雷要求妈妈让自己去玩一会儿。他兴奋地告诉妈妈晓菲和成成辩论的结果，妈妈**担心**他也会像晓菲一样被成成弄得 无话可说 ，但罗雷自信地说不可能。

　　成成在家准备明天的辩论赛，桌子上的**纸条**一条条地写着罗雷的缺点。成成妈妈也在帮忙演练，她教成成必须把罗雷的统治者管理方式作为辩论的重点，并且要告诉同学们他当班长与罗雷当班长的 不同之处 ：他会做班级的管理者，而不是统治者，他会协助老师、爱护 他人 。另一边，罗雷爸爸也在帮助罗雷**分析**辩论赛，并预测成成会对罗雷提出的问题，例如：罗雷打人。然而谈到这里，罗雷爸爸却认为罗雷打人没错。毕竟如果班长不严厉的话，很多同学都不会**听话**。

　　在辩论场上，成成首先说，他会成为班级的管理者，而不是统治者。他清楚地表明了管理者需要承担的责任，并让被罗雷打过的同学举手。两位候选人在辩论中 针锋相对 ，针对彼此的弱点相互指责。辩论结束后，成成在回家的路上与继父讲述了今天他与罗雷的辩论，他觉得自己 略胜一筹 。

Activity 1 Select the alternative explanation for the highlighted section.

Ⓐ 别人　　Ⓑ 更好　　Ⓒ 没有什么话可以说　　Ⓓ 不一样的地方　　Ⓔ 对立

1 妈妈担心罗雷会被成成弄得 无话可说 。_____

2 成成告诉同学们他当班长与罗雷当班长的 不同之处 。_____

3 两位候选人在辩论中 针锋相对 。_____

4 成成觉得自己 略胜一筹 。_____

5 成成说他会协助老师、爱护 他人 。_____

Activity 2 What are the characteristics of a class dictator and a class manager when managing a classroom? Write down their traits.

Ⓐ 打人　　　　Ⓑ 爱护同学　　　Ⓒ 拉人　　　　Ⓓ 态度严厉　　　Ⓔ 让同学们听话
Ⓕ 和同学平等相处　Ⓖ 关心帮助同学　Ⓗ 跟同学打架　Ⓘ 协助老师

统治者的特点	管理者的特点

(Extension) 你认为当班长还需要具备什么其他的特质？

_____

_____

_____

_____

场景分析

Activity 3 Circle the appropriate answer to complete the analysis.

　　导演使用蒙太奇 / 长镜头的手法呈现罗雷和成成与父母一起准备辩论赛的过程，这样的剪辑手法使观众更能感受到一家人 / 两家人的激烈竞争。

　　辩论赛的前一天，我们看到两位候选人**充满**信心 / 伤心的表现。例如，罗雷在公园里跟妈妈说他不可能像晓菲一样被成成弄得 无话可说 。下一个画面中，我们又看到成成正在认真地做着明天辩论赛要用的作业 / **笔记**。导演通过特写镜头 / 半身镜头 / 全身镜头使观众清楚地看到小纸条上写满了他收集 / **偷**到的罗雷的优点 / 缺点，显示出成成对辩论赛的**充分** / 不足准备。成成跟妈妈说如果自己把罗雷比下去，同学会百分之百**愿意**投票给他。通过近景镜头 / 全景镜头 / 半身镜头，我们看到成成充满自信的表情。

辩论赛前，导演拍到两位候选人的互动。可以看到罗雷和成成一起去了厕所，两人互相<u>开玩笑 / 争执</u>，取笑对方。这里看不到辩论前的紧张感，只看到两位候选人<u>天真可爱 / 成熟</u>稳重孩童的一面。

两位候选人被老师请到台上，通过<u>全景镜头 / 近景镜头 / 中景镜头</u>，我们再次看到教室墙上的"诚实勇敢，好学多思"八个大字，这也是学校对孩子们的<u>期许 / 想法</u>。成成先上场，向大家**陈述**了当班长需要具备的**特质**。当成成说到"被罗雷打过的人举手"时，镜头转向罗雷，我们可以看到他脸上<u>忽然 / 一直</u>出现了不自信的表情。但罗雷马上反问成成，"如果要选一位优秀的班长，你会选谁？"罗雷的问题让成成<u>想 / 笑</u>了一下。罗雷以一句"班长**必须**诚实"让成成无法回嘴。在这里，我们看到教室外的罗雷爸爸流露出开心的表情。

在整场辩论中，我们可以看到罗雷和成成都做着父母让他们做的事，说着父母要他们说的话。最后，成成形容罗雷是"统治者"的**样子** / 画面令罗雷 无话可说 。

Activity	4	Observe the family activities on the night before the debate competition between Cheng Cheng and Luo Lei and record your answers in the table.

	辩论前一晚
场　　景	
地　　点	＿＿＿＿＿＿＿＿＿＿＿＿　　　　＿＿＿＿＿＿＿＿＿＿＿＿
拍摄手法	＿＿＿＿＿＿＿＿＿＿＿＿　　　　＿＿＿＿＿＿＿＿＿＿＿＿
父母分别对他们说了什么？	

成成妈妈：

＿＿＿＿＿＿＿＿＿＿＿＿＿＿＿

＿＿＿＿＿＿＿＿＿＿＿＿＿＿＿

罗雷爸爸：

＿＿＿＿＿＿＿＿＿＿＿＿＿＿＿

＿＿＿＿＿＿＿＿＿＿＿＿＿＿＿

Support

A 明天一定要把这几句背下来。

B 管理就要管得严厉！

C 你要说要做一个班里的管理者，不是统治者。

D 你做班长和罗雷绝对不同。

E 明天你一定要问这个问题！

F 为什么打人？因为孩子不听话。

Prepare a presentation using the information from the table. You may begin with：

辩论前一晚，两方的父母都积极地为孩子第二天的辩论做准备。

You must include the following info in your presentation：

- 拍摄手法

- 为什么这样说？

- 父母对孩子们说了什么？

- 孩子们的态度／反应怎么样？

Activity 5 Observe Cheng Cheng and Luo Lei's debate performance and record your answers in the table.

场　　景		
地　　点	学校	学校
拍摄手法		
他们分别说了什么来攻击对方？		
成成：		罗雷：

Support

A 我要做班级的管理者，不会去做班级的统治者。

B 你还说你不管怎么样都会选我。

C 现在要选一个班长，你选谁？

D 挨过罗雷打的请举手。

E 管理者就是和同学和平相处，关心同学。

F 我可以改进我的管理方法。

G 有的大人还打小孩儿。

H 你是个骗子！当好班长必须诚实。

Activity 6 You are invited to be the judge for three candidates' debate competitions. Complete the following evaluation form. According to the following criteria, give a tick under the candidate who performed the best.

	晓菲	成成	罗雷
辩论 有理有据			
表达能力			
反驳能力			
风度 / 举止			
自信			

Now you need to comment on the performances of the three candidates and explain the reasons. You can start the sentence with...

从两场辩论赛中，我们可以看到…… / 就三位候选人的表现，我们发现……

_____

_____

_____

_____

_____

三位候选人的最后冲刺

35:09—41:42

大意

　　正式投票前，三位候选人还有一次演讲的机会，可以为自己拉票。父母也积极地和孩子一起准备第二天的演讲。晓菲的妈妈为晓菲写了**演讲稿**，晓菲看到一整张纸的演讲稿就哭了，妈妈则努力**安慰**她。成成的继父也用了一下午的时间帮成成写了演讲稿，成成觉得自己无法**背**下演讲稿的所有内容，于是他大声地骂人。罗雷爸爸也在教导罗雷如何演讲，怎么做**手势**，罗雷则是安静地听着爸爸的建议。爸爸还为罗雷准备了小礼物，第二天要送给同学们。

　　演讲的当天，成成首先上台，他**真诚**地**讲述**着自己会做一位有责任感的民主班长。第二位上台的是晓菲，晓菲先是礼貌地向大家问好，随后告诉大家虽然自己有过想放弃的想法，但是她希望自己能用更**出色**的表现**回报**同学。最后上台的是罗雷，他表现出了自信的态度，一字一句大声地背出演讲稿，说他愿意以服务者的态度管理班级。最后，他给所有同学和老师都送上了爸爸帮他准备的中秋节卡片。晓菲愉快地收下了卡片，然而成成拿到卡片以后，表情看起来不太开心。

Activity　1　**Connect the first half of the sentence with its corresponding second half.**

1　晓菲看到一整张纸的演讲稿就哭了，

2　成成觉得自己无法背下演讲稿的所有内容，

3　晓菲愉快地收下卡片，然而成成拿到卡片以后，表情看起来不太开心，

4　罗雷安静地听着爸爸的建议，

5　罗雷给所有同学和老师送上了爸爸帮他准备的中秋节卡片，

6　成成真诚地讲述着自己会做一位有责任感的民主班长，

A　他担心可能会影响投票的结果。

B　因为她觉得自己背不下来。

C　同学们看上去都兴奋极了。

D　跟之前不想父母帮忙的态度 截然不同 。

E　所以他开始对妈妈生气。

F　让大家相信他的决心。

Activity 2 Select the alternative explanation for the highlighted section.

> Ⓐ 说谢谢   Ⓑ 失去控制   Ⓒ 离开   Ⓓ 感受到很大的压力
>
> Ⓔ 大不相同   Ⓕ 能力不相上下   Ⓖ 最后的努力   Ⓗ 做一个榜样

1 晓菲已经开始 倍感压力 。_____

2 成成和妈妈说话说到一半，开始对妈妈生气，叫妈妈 滚 。_____

3 我们都看到成成和晓菲的情绪因为练习演讲的压力开始 失控 。_____

4 他们彼此都是 势均力敌 的对手。_____

5 罗雷搭配着手势向同学们介绍自己、问好以及 道谢 。_____

6 学校老师和家长都需要 以身作则 。_____

7 三位候选人在做 最后冲刺 。_____

8 罗雷现在的态度跟之前的 截然不同 。_____

场景分析

在《请投我一票》中，导演**偶尔**会穿插一些学生做团体活动和上课的画面。例如，在一节语文课上，大家一起朗读给演讲者的建议，其中一条"只要不害怕，心情就不会太紧张"预告着 即将到来 的候选人演讲。

妈妈在**办公室**说她**按照**晓菲的想法写了一篇演讲稿，晓菲看到妈妈写的长长的演讲稿就开始哭泣，妈妈则对她说"还没开始，你怎么知道自己不行？"这段画面显示出晓菲 倍感压力 。

画面转到成成家，我们先看到成成的父母拿着帮成成准备的演讲稿。成成妈妈担心演讲稿中"小孩子的语言太少"，成成无法背下来，同学们也听不懂。导演利用近景镜头拍摄成成没穿衣服**躺**在沙发上，看起来有一些**疲劳**。成成和妈妈说话说到一半，突然开始对妈妈生气，叫妈妈 滚 。

通过这几个画面，我们看到成成和晓菲的情绪因为练习演讲的压力而开始 失控 。这似乎不是八岁的孩子能承受的压力。比起另外两位候选人，罗雷显得比较自信，但是他的态度也在逐渐转变。整个晚上他都在听着爸爸的指导，并接受了爸爸的安排，准备给同学们送礼物。

画面又转到学校，我们看到一群小朋友在走廊上喊着口号"学会做人，学会学习，学会生活，诚实勇敢"，暗示着小朋友接受良好的品德教育的重要性，以及在这个过程中，学校老师和家长都需要 以身作则 。

演讲前，通过给到候选人表情的镜头，我们可以感受到成成和罗雷的紧张情绪。他们两位都没有百分之百的信心可以赢得这场选举，因为双方是 势均力敌（＝旗鼓相当）的对手。演讲的时候，成成和晓菲看着稿子真诚地讲述自己当上班长后的计划。罗雷上台后，搭配着手势向同学们问好、自我介绍并 道谢，整个过程没看演讲稿。最后送礼物的时候，罗雷还不**忘**给晓菲、成成和老师一份。成成发现同学们拿到罗雷送的卡片后非常开心，通过中景镜头，我们注意到这时候成成的表情看起来不太开心。

Activity 3 Discuss and fill in the table.

班长候选人	罗雷	成成	晓菲
身份	现任班长	下任班长候选人之一	升旗仪式司仪
性格优点			
性格缺点			
选举过程中性格有无变化？有什么样的变化？	有 / 无	有 / 无	有 / 无
有什么样的竞争优势？	1. 罗雷当过三年班长（现任班长）。 2. 父亲在武汉当地有权有势。	1. 妈妈提供各种各样的建议。 2. _____	1. 妈妈是学校行政人员。 2. _____
和父母有什么样的关系？举例说明。			
父母对他们说过什么话？	1. 打人是因为孩子不听话。 2. _____	1. 你和他竞选不能服输！ 2. 不能退出！	1. 要以理服人。 2. _____
当上班长后有什么计划？			

投票开始与结果公布

41:43—44:40

大意

　　演讲结束后，老师先告诉同学们选举的**规则**，提醒大家拿到**选票**后要认真思考，想清楚哪位候选人才是最好的选择，每个人都要在选票上勾选出自己支持的班长。大家填写完选票后，三位同学开始**唱票**，班上的同学看起来都很期待。随着选票一张张展开，罗雷的票数越来越多。最终的选举**结果**是：罗雷 25 票，成成 8 票，许晓菲 6 票。老师宣布罗雷当选为新班长。成成因为选举失败跑到教室外面哭了。晓菲的妈妈也安慰了哭泣的晓菲。班主任肯定了晓菲和成成的**艰苦**努力，并说选举的结果不重要，最重要的是他们的选举经历。她让成成、晓菲跟罗雷**握手**，向新班长表示祝贺。

　　班长选举**终于**结束了，老师让班上同学从现在开始听罗雷的指挥。

> **The cultural highlight**
> Chinese tally marks
> 一 丁 下 正 正

Activity 1 Write the meaning of the following phrases in English.

票
投票 to vote
拉票 _____
选票 _____
唱票 _____
票数 _____

出
表达出 _____
表现出 _____
传达出 _____
凸显出 _____
流露出 _____
显现出 _____

景
中景 _____
近景 _____
全景 _____
远景 _____

导

引导 _____

指导 _____

教导 _____

疲

疲劳 _____

疲倦 _____

疲惫 _____

击

攻击 _____

打击 _____

反击 _____

陪

陪伴 _____

陪同 _____

态

态度 _____

心态 _____

互

互相 _____

相互 _____

感

感觉 _____

感受 _____

用

利用 _____

使用 _____

运用 _____

身

半身镜头 _____

全身镜头 _____

照

按照 _____

照着 _____

果

成果 _____

结果 _____

安

安慰 _____

安抚 _____

权

权益 _____

权力 _____

权利 _____

歉

道歉 _____

抱歉 _____

指

指示 _____

指出 _____

指挥 _____

选

选择 _____

候选人 _____

落选 _____

选举 _____

勾选 _____

选票 _____

当选 _____

参选 _____

助选 _____

场景分析

Activity 2 Circle the appropriate answer to complete the analysis.

　　导演以不同的镜头表现方式真实地记录了投票 / 选票及票数 / 开票的过程，在这个过程中，我们看到有人 手舞足蹈 ，也有人为了选举结果 / 成果难过哭泣。

　　投票开始前，白板 / 黑板上已经写好了"竞选班长 / 班长投票"和三位候选人的姓名。导演以半身镜头拍摄老师对同学们说"我的班长我做主，我的票房 / 选票我做主"，强调同学们应该认真思考，然后投下自己神圣 / 难得的一票。

　　投票开始的时候，在画面中我们看到小朋友们 小心翼翼 地勾选 / 圈选了自己支持的候选人的名字，导演也特别拍摄了晓菲和罗雷的言行 / 表情，晓菲的表情不如罗雷的看起来有自信、有把握，而是多了一点儿从容 / 紧张。

　　唱票的时候，导演用了近景镜头拍摄三位候选人的面部表情。当罗雷的票一张张开出来的时候，有人开始说"罗雷赢定了 / 输定了！"一些小朋友也开始跟罗雷握手表示**恭喜**。画面中我们可以看到，成成的表情越来越凝重 / **骄傲**。

　　罗雷最后以 25 票高票当选下一任班长。之后我们看到成成跑到教室外难过地大哭。即使在选举过程中成成的态度 / 言行像个大人一样，但是他和晓菲仍然是小孩子，输了 / 赢了竞选后他们就像孩子一样 毫无掩饰 地表现出难过的心情。最后，三位候选人也在老师的建议下互相握手 / 牵手、拥抱，展现出了"君子之争"的**风度**。

　　在影片的最后一个画面中，我们可以看到罗雷神气 / 自卑地走在队伍中，成成在后面盯着罗雷。从这个画面我们可以看出，一旦罗雷班长做得不好，在下次班长选举中，大家又会再选出新的班长来欣赏 / 取代罗雷。

Activity 3 Complete the following paragraph about 君子之争.

Ⓐ 民族	Ⓑ 之间	Ⓒ 竞争	Ⓓ 善良	Ⓔ 选举
Ⓕ 互动	Ⓖ 尊重	Ⓗ 保持	Ⓘ 态度	Ⓙ 孔子

什么是君子之争？

　　在 _____ 看来，君子 _____ 的 _____ 要建立在"礼"之上，即使是 _____ ，也必须 _____ 纯正、_____ 的 _____ 。因此在最后，老师让成成、晓菲 _____ 这次 _____ 的结果，一起祝贺罗雷。这是中华 _____ 的美德。

| Activity | 4 | If you were a school teacher, how would you explain the concept of 君子之争 to the candidates for the next class monitor election? |

_____

_____

_____

_____

_____

_____

Chapter

4

Characters Analysis

主角分析：许晓菲

Xu Xiaofei is one of three candidates running for the position of a class monitor in the documentary *Please Vote for Me*, and she is the only female candidate. Xiaofei was brought up in a single-parent family. Although her family cannot provide the financial and other interventions that the other two candidates have, she does have a mother who always carefully supports her. When she heard the teacher announce that she had been chosen as a candidate for the class monitor, her face was both nervous and excited. Being chosen by a group of teachers to compete for class monitor was clearly a form of confirmation for her.

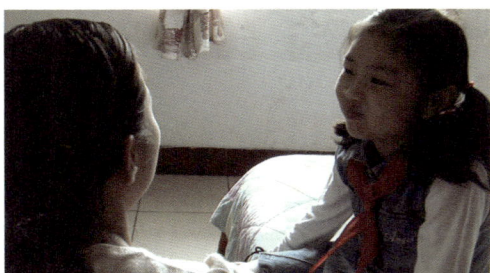

Xiaofei is well-mannered, friendly, and obedient, with a cute and bashful grin on her face most of the time. Her words and behaviour are respectful, making her an excellent role model for others to look up to. However, Xiaofei is quite timid, introverted, and lacks confidence when compared to the two lively and extroverted boys. She frequently relies on her mother's gentle support to gather the courage to participate in campaign activities. It is evident from her conversations with her mother that Xiaofei struggles to express herself verbally and lacks independent thinking. She ponders attentively for a considerable time when her mother discusses campaigning for the class monitor and seeks her opinion, but she still hopes for direct guidance from her mother, unlike the two boys who enthusiastically engage in discussions with their parents about their own ideas. It is apparent that Xiaofei's resilience is not as robust as the other two boys.

When she stood on stage and was constantly mocked and booed by the boys, she began crying and felt bewildered and was unable to fight back. Based on the traumatised reaction, it is possible to deduce that Xiaofei's prospects for election appear bleak. However, she received sympathy and support from her female classmates.

Nevertheless, the election experience had a significant impact on Xiaofei's personality growth. She gained confidence and courage to tackle challenges, and she learnt to take personal responsibility over time. Xiaofei became more assertive in her arguments with her opponent due to the discussion with her mother and the campaign tactics she prepared. Despite not winning the election, Xiaofei learnt valuable lessons from the experience and accepted the outcome gracefully.

Activity 1 According to your understanding of Xiaofei, complete the table below with relevant information.

(Extension) 用中文在班上做一个介绍晓菲的小型演讲，演讲时请使用下面这些表达。

	句型	Write your answers below in English. Extension: Write in Chinese.
个人信息	晓菲是…… 晓菲来自……家庭 她是唯一的…… 晓菲的参选**动机** / 原因是……	Eg She is the only female candidate.
服装	晓菲总是穿着…… 晓菲戴着……	
样子	晓菲看起来…… 她常常表现出……	Eg She looks naive.
性格	她的性格是……的 既……又…… 不但……而且…… 特别…… 缺乏…… 尽管晓菲……，但是……	Eg She sometimes lacks confidence.
家庭与人际关系	晓菲和 _____ 的关系很…… 晓菲和 _____ 相处得……	
外在影响	晓菲受到 _____ 的影响，所以……	
晓菲的成长	选举过程中…… 选举结束后…… 晓菲变得 + adj. 晓菲成为 + noun 晓菲转变成 + noun	

Activity 2 Based on the film, choose the most appropriate word in the box to fill in the blanks.

> (A) 支持　　(B) **显得**　　(C) 留下　　(D) 面对　　(E) 来自
>
> (F) **喝倒彩**　　(G) 缺少　　(H) 哭泣　　(I) 流露出　　(J) 拿出

1 晓菲 _____ 一个单亲家庭。

2 晓菲有一位总是默默 _____ 她的母亲。

3 在听到老师说自己成为班长候选人的时候，晓菲的脸上 _____ 既紧张又兴奋的表情。

4 跟两位**活泼外向**的男孩子相比，晓菲 _____ **害羞**、内向又 _____ 自信。

5 在母亲的鼓励下，晓菲 _____ 了**勇气**参加班长竞选活动。

6 晓菲站在讲台上的时候被男同学大声地**嘲笑**，因此她开始不停地 _____ 。

7 根据影片内容，晓菲在竞选时期与全班同学没有太多的互动，因此她没有给大家 _____ **深刻**的印象。

8 晓菲太**在意**别人对她的看法，容易受压力影响，而且没有勇气去 _____ **挫折**。

9 成成**说服**晓菲和他一起对罗雷的表演 _____ 。

Activity 3 Highlight the false description about Xiaofei and then rewrite each sentence in Chinese.

1 晓菲从妈妈那里得到了**足够**的经济帮助，而她妈妈也**干涉**了班长竞选。(hint: 2 mistakes)

_____

2 晓菲的言行和态度都很没礼貌、不**正直**，所以她不是一个**值得**大家学习的**对象**。(hint: 2 mistakes)

_____

3 从晓菲和母亲的对话中，我们可以发现她**善于**表达而且很有**主见**。(hint: 2 mistakes)

_____

4 和另外两个男孩子一样，晓菲热情地和母亲讨论她的想法，不希望母亲给她建议。(hint: 3 mistakes)

_____

5 一开始和妈妈在家中的卧室一起讨论如何展示才艺表演的时候，我们看到的晓菲是一个又**大方**又有自信的女孩儿。(hint: 2 mistakes)

_____

6 晓菲最后没有上台完成才艺表演，由此可见晓菲是一个不负责的学生。(hint: 2 mistakes)

_____

Activity 4 Use the quotes from Xiaofei suggested below to fill in the blanks. You don't have to use the exact words.

A 我不敢……

B 要是我说错了……

C 可是三年级的时候我也改了啊！

D **收集**……的缺点交给我。

E 即使有了困难，也应该勇敢面对，不能过分依赖他人。

F 罗雷，罗雷，**威胁**别人。

晓菲的重点场景
尽管晓菲为才艺表演做了**充分**的准备，但是在要上台前还是跟母亲说"＿＿＿＿＿"，透露出她对自己没有信心。
成成想说服晓菲一起给罗雷的表演喝倒彩，但是她说"＿＿＿＿＿"。从这里我们可以看出晓菲天性天真、善良又胆小。
罗雷表演完后，晓菲加入了成成，和一群同学一起对着罗雷大声说"＿＿＿＿＿"。表示晓菲从这里开始转变，和以前的天真性格形成了**对比**。
在辩论前，晓菲叫她的小助手们去＿＿＿＿＿。从这里我们可以**确定**她价值观的改变，想和其他候选人一样做**负面**的反击。

（续表）

	晓菲的重点场景
	在辩论的时候，虽然成成说晓菲太爱哭了，所以不能够当班长，但是晓菲却**坚定**地说"＿＿＿＿＿＿"。这里反映出晓菲的成长，她变成了一位懂得勇敢反击的人。
	尽管晓菲没有当选班长，但是在最后的演讲中，她说到"＿＿＿＿＿＿"。这里反映出在**经历**过 一波三折 的挑战之后，她更加了解自己了。

一波三折： 用来描述事情进行中有许多困难和阻碍。

Activity 5

In the documentary, *Please Vote for Me*, the personality, family, growth, and transformation of Xiaofei are key focuses. Please read the following English passages and translate them into Chinese. As a challenge, discuss with your teacher if you have different perspectives before you write them down.

Xiaofei is a candidate who is quiet and obedient, and also relatively timid. Compared to the other two candidates, she is less confident in herself. After finding out that she is one of the candidates for the class monitor, she seems to be excited but feeling a little nervous.

Xiaofei is afraid of conflict and dislikes attacking others. She felt nervous when facing pressure from her classmates. During the process of this election, Xiaofei had moments of sadness and fear. However, with her mother's help, she learnt to bravely face her opponents.

Xiaofei has a close relationship with her mother. She often shares her worries with her mother, who also cares deeply about her. Her mother's support is crucial for Xiaofei when facing difficulties.

Although Xiaofei did not win the election at the end, she seemed to accept defeat better than Cheng Cheng. This election's experience has made Xiaofei stronger than she was before.

(grid writing space)

Activity 6 Use a dictionary to look up the meanings of the following idioms. Review the timestamp in the video provided, then write a few sentences using the specified idiom to describe the scene with Xiaofei.

惊慌
失措

▶ Watch from 8:50

► Watch from 9:30

泪如
雨下

► Watch from 10:52

半途
而废

► Watch from 21:12

忐忑
不安

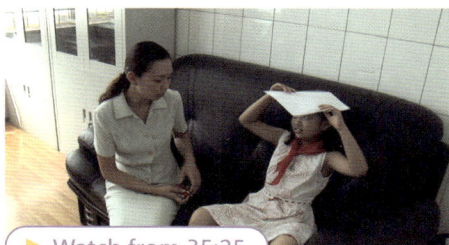

► Watch from 35:25

七上
八下

► Watch from 39:37

不懈
努力

主角分析：成成

Cheng Cheng is one of the two male candidates competing in this class monitor election.

His confidence was unshakeable when being called on stage by his teacher hearing he had been chosen. With an innate aptitude for leadership, he was certain that he would receive widespread approval from his classmates.

Cheng Cheng is confident, outgoing, and always thoughtful. For his talent show, he chose a famous song of the time to sing, in order for it to resonate with the class. Always keen to showcase his abilities, he also demonstrated a keen awareness of his audience, engaging with them to create a dynamic atmosphere. In his election campaign, he rehearsed with his assistants in an empty classroom and sought advice from his parents, perfecting every movement and sentence he would deliver on stage.

He is also shrewd and cunning. He did not hesitate to employ tactics to counter his opponents during his campaign. He successfully provoked his classmates to heckle Xiaofei during her performance, capitalising on her flaws. He also capitalised on the general dissatisfaction with Luo Lei's authoritarian style, gathering evidence against him that resulted in a decline in Luo Lei's support. He made it clear to his classmates that the class needed a "manager" rather than a "ruler". He advocated for democratic harmony, rejecting the idea of dictatorial leadership from the current class monitor, Luo Lei. The election meant a lot to him. It is evident that when Luo Lei's father took the entire class on a monorail ride and distributed gifts, he felt a surge of anxiety, fearing that it would influence his votes.

At home, Cheng Cheng frequently discussed the election with his parents and kept them up to date on relevant news. Cheng Cheng is the family's only child. Apart from having high hopes for him, his parents lavish attention on him in their daily lives, meeting his needs from food to entertainment. His mother, who works at a local TV station, taught him the art of eloquent speech and both parents helped him with writing his final speech. His parents gave him advice and shared their thoughts, assisting his development from a young boy to an amateur "politician", who enjoyed strategic tactics and the taste of power. Cheng Cheng is clearly regarded as a treasured and spoiled "little emperor" in his household. While his election campaign was exhausting, he shouted at his mother, demanding she leave the room. His mother,

on the other hand, remained calm and patient, emphasising that becoming class monitor was a steppingstone to larger leadership roles, comparing it to China's former president, Hu Jintao.

Despite his best efforts, Cheng Cheng found it difficult to accept his defeat when the final results were announced. With his dreams shattered, he struggled to meet the gaze of the newly elected class monitor, Luo Lei. His inflated pride made accepting defeat to Luo Lei a difficult pill to swallow.

Activity 1 According to your understanding of Cheng Cheng, complete the table below with the relevant information.

Extension Make a mini presentation to introduce Cheng Cheng in Chinese to your class using the provided language

	句型	Write your answers below in English. Extension: Write in Chinese.
个人信息	成成是…… 成成来自……家庭 他觉得自己…… 成成的参选动机 / 原因是……	Eg He felt that he would be favoured by everyone.
服装	成成总是穿着…… 成成戴着…… 成成在家常常……	

（续表）

	句型	Write your answers below in English. Extension: Write in Chinese.
样子	成成看起来…… 他常常表现出……	Eg He is frequently manipulative.
性格	他的性格是……的 既……又…… 不但……而且…… 特别…… 缺乏…… 尽管成成……，但是……	Eg His personality is dishonest and stubborn.
家庭与 人际关系	成成和 _____ 的关系很…… 成成和 _____ 相处得……	
外在影响	成成受到 _____ 的影响， 所以……	
成成的成长	选举过程中…… 选举结束后…… 成成变得 + adj. 成成成为 + noun 成成转变成 + noun	

Activity 2 Based on the film, choose the most appropriate word in the box to fill in the blanks.

Ⓐ 宠坏	Ⓑ 暗示	Ⓒ 有关	Ⓓ 接受	Ⓔ 充满
Ⓕ 能够	Ⓖ 需要	Ⓗ 成为	Ⓘ 讨论	Ⓙ **提出**

1 当成成听到自己成为候选人的时候，他 _____ 自信地走到台上。

2 成成不仅会利用机会好好展现自己，而且还 _____ 同时注意台下**观众**的反应。

3 他 _____ 的 "政见（political view）" 很不错，清楚地跟同学说明了班级 _____ 的是一个 "管理者"，而不是 "统治者"。

4 在家里的场景中，我们看到成成对他的母亲非常没礼貌，对她 大呼小叫 。从这里不难看出，在家中他就是一个被父母 _____ 了的小孩儿，跟"小皇帝"一样。

5 当成成想退出班长竞选的时候，他的母亲说服他**继续**，并 _____ 说如果他将来想 _____ 国家领导人，第一步就是要当班长。

6 成成喜欢和他的父母 _____ 班长选举的**话题**，也爱和他们讲（说）与竞选 _____ 的**消息**。

7 宣布投票结果之后，成成无法 _____ 失败，因为他为这次选举下了很多**功夫**。

大呼小叫： 形容人激动或夸张地表达自己的情绪或意见。

Activity 3 Highlight the false description about Cheng Cheng and then rewrite each sentence in Chinese.

1 才艺表演的时候，我们可以看到成成说话的样子很没自信，充满了担心与害怕。(hint: 2 mistakes)

_____

2 如果成成当上班长，他不想用民主的方式和大家 和睦相处 ，而是想要"**统治**"班级。(hint: 2 mistakes)

_____

3 受学校教育的影响，成成 能言善道 ，老师也教他竞争的方法与手段，希望他能积极向上，成为新班长。(hint: 2 mistakes)

_____

4 成成和父母不太重视这次班长选举，他们认为只要成成开心就好。(hint: 2 mistakes)

_____

5 成成的母亲在学校工作，她训练成成唱歌和演讲的技巧，甚至帮他写了一首歌。(hint: 2 mistakes)

_____

6 在宣布班长选举结果之后，成成不但没有哭，而且还开心地接受自己**输**给了罗雷。(hint: 2 mistakes)

_____

和睦相处： 指人们之间友好和谐地相处。
能言善道： 指一个人口才很好，擅长用语言表达自己的想法和观点。

Activity 4 Use the quotes from Cheng Cheng suggested below to fill in the blanks. You don't have to use the exact words.

Ⓐ 民主到底是什么意思？

Ⓑ 罗雷，罗雷，最爱打人！

Ⓒ 我代表罗雷向你**道歉**。

Ⓓ 再去采访那个女孩儿一次。

Ⓔ 打倒晓菲！

Ⓕ 起哄说表演得不好。

Ⓖ 这是统治者，不是班长。

Ⓗ 当班长都是以身作则的！

Ⓘ 我妈昨天告诉我一个招数。

Ⓙ 你要是投我，我让你当学习**委员**。

Ⓚ 班长就有**权力**。

	成成的重点场景
	在影片的开头，成成跟继父说"＿＿＿＿＿＿"，这显示出他想当管理者的原因。
	从一开始成成问继父"＿＿＿＿＿＿"，我们可以知道他并不了解老师白天在班上说的"要进行一场民主的选举"是什么意思。
	为了**干扰**晓菲的才艺表演，成成跟朋友**串通**说"＿＿＿＿＿＿"。从这里我们看到他并不是一位正直的人。
	在晓菲表演时，成成**故意带头**在全班起哄说"＿＿＿＿＿＿"。这说明他知道如何利用晓菲的**弱点**去打击她。

（续表）

	成成的重点场景
	"打倒晓菲事件"是由成成**策划**的，但是看到晓菲哭了以后他却说"＿＿＿＿＿＿"，从这里可以知道成成是一个又有**心机**又不诚实的人。
	当罗雷要表演才艺的时候，成成兴奋地跟老师说"＿＿＿＿＿＿"，从这里我们可以看出家庭教育对小孩子言行的影响。
	成成在罗雷的才艺表演结束以后，带头跟同学一起起哄说"＿＿＿＿＿＿"，**由此可见**，他并没有从之前的"打倒晓菲"事件中学到**教训**。
	成成知道如何贿赂投票的人，他会通过给别人好处和职位来获得支持，成成甚至跟人说"＿＿＿＿＿＿"。
	成成在辩论的时候对晓菲说"＿＿＿＿＿＿"，但是他自己却没有说到做到，而且还贿赂同学，带头起哄。
	成成的性格不容易相信别人，**比如**他跟导演说"＿＿＿＿＿＿"，因为他不相信同学会当着他的面说**实话**。
	在辩论的时候，成成知道大家很不欣赏罗雷的管理方式，所以对他说"＿＿＿＿＿＿"，让大家对罗雷的支持率**下降**，影响罗雷的心情。

Activity 5 In the documentary, *Please Vote for Me*, Cheng Cheng's personality, behaviour, family, and election strategy are key focuses. Please read the following English passages and translate into Chinese. As a challenge, discuss with your teacher if you have different perspectives before you write them down.

Cheng Cheng is a smart student but sometimes his behaviour is immature. Before the election, he was unfamiliar with democratic elections and even asked his stepfather, "What is democracy?" Afterwards, he gradually becomes more determined to win the election and starts employing various negative tactics and strategies.

He not only plotted the "bring down Xiaofei" incident but also used methods suggested by his mother to attack Luo Lei. In his talent performance, he lets friends support him on stage and interacted with classmates. In order to get more votes, he even bribed a classmate in exchange for a deputy monitor position.

Cheng Cheng is the pampered "little emperor" of his family, adored by his mother. She not only fulfils his demands but also helps him think of solutions to his problems. During Luo Lei's performance, his mother advised him to boo.

In the debate competition, he prepared his opponent's shortcomings; for example, Luo Lei's dictatorship behaviour and Xiaofei's lack of confidence.

However, when he found out he lost the election, he cried like a little child, showing that his weakness is inability to accept defeats.

Activity 6 Use a dictionary to look up the meanings of the following idioms. Review the timestamp in the video provided, then write a few sentences using the specified idiom to describe the scene with Cheng Cheng.

没大
没小

出言
不逊

▶ Watch from 6:52

偷偷
摸摸

▶ Watch from 8:09

Watch from 13:54

沾沾
自喜

Watch from 17:29

手舞
足蹈

Watch from 19:30

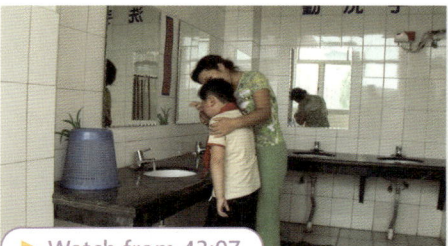

愁眉
不展

Watch from 43:07

号啕
大哭

主角分析：罗雷

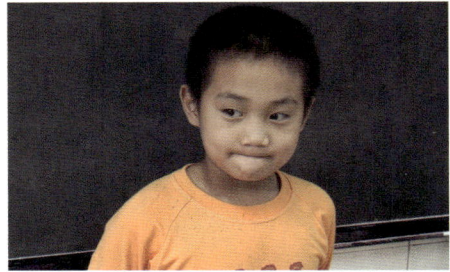

In the documentary, *Please Vote for Me*, Luo Lei is the current class monitor and one of three candidates for this election. At the beginning, he is self-assured that he is the best candidate for the job and that the other two candidates cannot compete with him because he has the experience of being a class monitor for two years. However, he is not a natural leader. He was shown as a child that managing children required strong and firm approaches. He enjoys privileges as class monitor and has an intimidating attitude, even resorting to bullying and physical violence towards disobedient or disruptive classmates.

For example, when tension erupts between Luo Lei and his classmates during a lunch break, he shouts to those who challenge him, believing that this is what leadership means. Immediately after the election, he forgot all the promises he made during the campaign and quickly reverted to his re-election attitude, asking the person who could not keep silence to stand in front for punishment, a form of corporal punishment.

Luo Lei believes that physical force is more effective than having a conversation in getting his classmates to listen to him. However, these behaviours become his electoral weakness. During the talent show, his classmates make fun of him for his reputation for violence and express their displeasure with him. Cheng Cheng seizes the opportunity to rally the class against him. A student tells the director that he would not vote for Luo Lei because he frequently punches others, demonstrating the strained connection between Luo Lei and his classmates. Luo Lei tries to find out who will vote for him in another scene, but a boy refuses. Luo Lei becomes dismayed after realising he is not as popular as Cheng Cheng and decides to withdraw from the election.

Luo Lei's election triumph is largely due to his parents' use of their influence to intervene and advise him. He accepts his father's offer to invite the entire class on a school trip to take the monorail, knowing that the kids will enjoy it. His father also prepares Mid-Autumn Festival cards and reminds Luo Lei to distribute to everyone before voting, which, we can assume, the children will naturally like, and the votes will flow towards Luo Lei despite his reputation. We also witness Luo Lei's poor attitude throughout the debate towards Cheng Cheng. He picked up on his father's teachings about " hitting people," which is not a good attitude for a primary school student.

The class monitor election exposed Luo Lei's transformation. During the flag-raising ceremony at the beginning of the film, we see Luo Lei as a brave and upright young boy. When he realised he was running for class monitor, he denied his parents' assistance and insisted on depending solely on his own true strength. Despite his parents' indoctrination, Luo Lei believed in his principles of "not controlling others" and "everyone can vote for whomever they want."

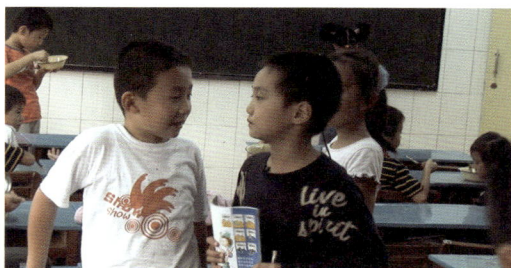

His faith was shaken, however, as he was subjected to taunting and mockery led by Cheng Cheng during his talent performance. He was publicly criticised for being an aggressive leader and then discovered that others refused to vote for him. His confidence was shattered afterwards, and he wanted to withdraw from the election.

At this low point, his parents intervened and used his father's connection to bribe the entire class into participating in a trip, and Luo Lei discovered that his popularity had been restored as a result of the bribe. This was also the tipping point that led Luo Lei to abandon fair competition in favour of corruption. In the final stage, he was determined to follow his father's orders without hesitation and to give gifts to the entire class in order to gain more support. The school motto includes the phrase "learn to be a human being", so perhaps what Luo Lei learnt from this election was how to use power to deal with the fickleness of human nature.

Activity 1 According to your understanding of Luo Lei, complete the table below with relevant information.

(Extension) Make a mini presentation to introduce Luo Lei in Chinese to your class using the provided language.

	句型	Write your answers below in English. Extension: Write in Chinese.
个人信息	罗雷是…… 罗雷来自……家庭 他是家中唯一的…… 罗雷想连任班长（继续做班长）的动机／原因是……	Eg He is the current class monitor.
服装	罗雷总是穿着…… 罗雷戴着……	
样子	罗雷看起来…… 他常常表现出……	Eg He seems very arrogant.
性格	他的性格是……的 既……又…… 不但……而且…… 特别…… 缺乏…… 尽管罗雷……，但是……	Eg He is always being harsh and bossy to his peers.
家庭与人际关系	罗雷和 _____ 的关系很…… 罗雷和 _____ 相处得……	
外在影响	罗雷受到 _____ 的影响，所以……	

（续表）

	句型	Write your answers below in English. Extension: Write in Chinese.
罗雷的转变	选举过程中…… 选举结束后…… 罗雷变得 + adj. 罗雷 + noun 罗雷转变成 + noun	

Activity 2 Based on the film, choose the most appropriate word in the box to fill in the blanks.

> Ⓐ 管理　　Ⓑ 意识　　Ⓒ 拒绝　　Ⓓ 表达　　Ⓔ 表现
> Ⓕ 作为　　Ⓖ 技巧　　Ⓗ 尝试　　Ⓘ 利用　　Ⓙ 造成影响

1️⃣ 在纪录片中，罗雷 ＿＿＿＿＿＿ 出很有自信而且很骄傲的样子。

2️⃣ 罗雷认为自己才是最**适合**当班长的人，另外两位候选人**似乎**无法对他 ＿＿＿＿＿＿ 。

3️⃣ 在班上，＿＿＿＿＿＿ 班长的他享有特权，对同学的态度 咄咄逼人 ，甚至有霸凌行为。

4️⃣ 在操场的场景中，罗雷展现出严格而且有效的班级 ＿＿＿＿＿＿ 。

5️⃣ 在才艺表演中，同学们嘲笑罗雷打人，＿＿＿＿＿＿ 出大家对他的不满。

6️⃣ 在另一个场景中，罗雷 ＿＿＿＿＿＿ 去了解谁会投票给他，但是遭到了别人的拒绝。

7️⃣ 罗雷失望地 ＿＿＿＿＿＿ 到自己并不受欢迎，因此想要**退出**班长选举。

8️⃣ 罗雷这次当选班长有很大的原因是来自他父母的帮助和 ＿＿＿＿＿＿ 权力**干预**选举。

9️⃣ 罗雷一开始 ＿＿＿＿＿＿ 了父母的帮助，**坚持**靠自己真正的实力。

🔟 尽管父母尝试说服他用 "＿＿＿＿＿＿" 来竞选，但是罗雷一开始还是认为要 光明正大 ，不能去控制别人。

咄咄逼人：用来描述人的行为方式太强势霸道，不考虑别人感受。
光明正大：用来形容一个人或者行为非常诚实、公正。

Activity 3 Highlight the false description about Luo Lei and then rewrite each sentence in Chinese.

1 罗雷从来都没有当过班长，但 不可否认 的是，从父母那里学到的管理方法使他得到了大部分同学的**尊敬**。(hint: 2 mistakes)

_____

2 学校的教育让罗雷明白，想要管理好班上同学，就应该采用良好的沟通方式。(hint: 2 mistakes)

_____

3 在才艺表演之前，同学们嘲笑罗雷没自信，这反映出同学们看不起他。(hint: 2 mistakes)

_____

4 晓菲利用机会，引导班上同学给罗雷加油打气。(hint: 2 mistakes)

_____

5 同学跟导演说想投票给罗雷，因为罗雷经常帮助别人，这显示出罗雷和同学之间的友好关系。(hint: 3 mistakes)

_____

6 罗雷没有接受建议邀请全班参加轻轨旅游，因为他觉得这是在贿赂别人。(hint: 2 mistakes)

_____

不可否认： 用来强调一个事实或观点是无法否定或拒绝的。

Activity 4 Use the quotes from Luo Lei suggested below to fill in the blanks. You don't have to use the exact words.

A 你等一下说成成的缺点，说我的优点

B 我管得严，大家才会怕我

C 像你这样的孩子我必须严，不严你**绝对**不会听

D 说实话，我想退出选举

E 要想当好班长必须诚实

F 谁再讲话，就站到前面去

G 要靠真正的实力，不要控制别人

H 有的大人还打小孩儿呢

	罗雷的重点场景
	尽管罗雷的父母一开始给了他很多建议，但是他还是觉得 _____。这显示出他当了两年班长，对自己还是很有信心的。
	受到家长 潜移默化 的影响，罗雷管理班级的方法并不被人欣赏，他甚至还 义正词严 地对着一位男同学说"_____"。
	在与成成的辩论之后，罗雷第一次感受到 前所未有 的打击，所以他说"_____"。
	为了帮自己拉票，罗雷在辩论前跟同学说"_____"。
	辩论的时候，罗雷攻击成成说"_____"，但是罗雷自己做到了吗？
	受家庭教育的影响，罗雷在辩论的时候对成成说"_____"，来**解释**自己打人是**合理**的。
	当着全班的面，成成大声地告诉罗雷说全班都害怕当了两年班长的他，不过罗雷却解释说"_____"。由此可见，罗雷认为一个好领导是以力服人，而不是以理服人。

（续表）

罗雷的重点场景	
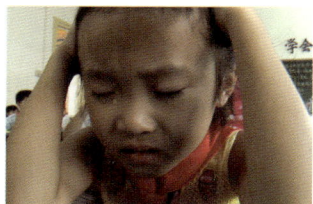	在辩论的时候，罗雷说他的管理方法不对，他会改，但是他一当选后，马上就想**体罚**别人，对同学说"＿＿＿＿＿＿＿"。

潜移默化： 指人的思想或性格受到其他方面的影响，不知不觉地发生了变化。
义正词严： 道理正当，措辞严肃。
前所未有： 是指一件事情或情况是从前没出现或经历过的。

Activity 5

In the documentary, *Please Vote for Me*, Luo Lei's personality, behaviour, family background, and election strategy are key focuses. Please read the following English passages and translate into Chinese. As a challenge, discuss with your teacher if you have different perspectives before writing down.

Luo Lei is a confident but arrogant current class monitor. He comes from a wealthy family, and his parents have high expectations of him. Initially, he seemed not to worry much about the election, even refusing his parents' help, telling them not to "control others". During the talent show, he displayed his multiple talents by both singing and playing the flute.

However, he gradually felt threatened by Cheng Cheng and realised that many classmates might not vote for him. This is because he was criticised for being a dictator and even "hit" people who did not listen to him. Therefore, he started to lose confidence and even considered withdrawing from the election.

Later, Luo Lei had no choice but to accept help from his parents. After the success of the monorail trip, he became more confident in his parents' advice. In the debate, he used his father's suggestions to attack Cheng Cheng and won the election by giving Mid-Autumn Festival cards, prepared by his father, to his classmates before voting. Throughout this election process, Luo Lei transformed from an independent-minded boy to one who solely listens and follows his parents' advice and depends on their help and support.

（写作方格）

Activity 6 Use a dictionary to look up the meanings of the following idioms. Review the timestamp in the video we provided, then write a few sentences using the specified idiom to describe the scene with Luo Lei.

▶ Watch from 4:04

胸有
成竹

火冒
三丈

▶ Watch from 16:11

心灰
意冷

愁眉
苦脸

▶ Watch from 17:00

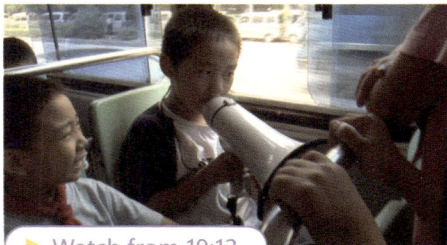 

乐在
其中

▶ Watch from 19:12

气急
败坏

恼羞
成怒

▶ Watch from 32:50

从容
不迫

▶ Watch from 40:27

Activity 7 Compare the three candidates and answer the following questions.

Discuss

1 请比较他们的外貌。

2 请比较他们的性格。

3 他们在班长选举中表现出了什么样的行为？出现了什么样的冲突？

4 他们之间的关系如何？

5 他们与自己家长的关系如何？

6 他们各自有哪些正面形象？

7 他们各自有哪些负面形象？

8 他们各自有哪些令你觉得有趣的地方？

9 他们有什么相同点？

10 他们有什么不同的地方？

UNIT 4

配角分析：张老师

Mrs. Zhang, a third-grade homeroom teacher (also known as form tutor), is one of the teachers that organised the inaugural democratic class monitor election in Class 1. Typically, this position was appointed by the teacher, but in this instance, students were given the chance to vote for their favoured leader.

Mrs. Zhang explained the procedure, but didn't extensively delve into the core principles and values of democracy. This lack of clarity resulted in confusion, with students like Cheng Cheng needing to consult their parents at home to understand the concept of democracy.

The documentary showed several incidents, such as Xiaofei and Luo Lei's talent show, where they faced ridicule or disparagement from their peers, including Cheng Cheng and Luo Lei. Mrs. Zhang did not intervene immediately but only stepped in when the students became visibly upset. Additionally, she failed to explicitly condemn such disruptive behaviour, even though she had prior knowledge of Cheng Cheng's intention to disrupt Luo Lei's performance.

When Cheng Cheng considered withdrawing because Luo Lei was getting more favoured by the class after the monorail trip, Mrs. Zhang responded firmly, advising him not to quit halfway. She did not offer consolation, suggesting a potential lack of emotional support for the students. It was only at the end of the voting process that she emphasised the importance of the experience and the learning process rather than focusing on the outcome.

The documentary implied that Zhang's intention was to facilitate a fair competition and help students comprehend democracy. However, there were evident disparities in the resources accessible to the candidates, and she did not prohibit Luo Lei from soliciting votes through gifts and a trip. Zhang could have made greater efforts to highlight the significance of integrity, fairness, and the avoidance of favouritism during the election, instead of inadvertently endorsing a "vote-buying" culture.

Activity 1 Based on the film, choose the most appropriate word in the box to fill in the blanks.

Ⓐ 鼓励　　Ⓑ 班长　　Ⓒ 放弃　　Ⓓ 领导
Ⓔ **班主任**　　Ⓕ 发表　　Ⓖ 选举

1 张老师是三年级一班的 _____，她也是策划这次班长 _____ 的人之一。

2 她一开始就跟全班说明通常 _____ 是由老师指派的。

3 张老师跟同学们说明"民主"就是由学生自己选出自己的 _____。

4 张老师**强调**班上的每一位同学都有 _____ 自己意见的**权利**。

5 张老师叫晓菲去教室外面休息一下，还 _____ 晓菲要勇敢。

6 但是当成成跟张老师说想要弃选的时候，老师却严肃地跟他说事情做到一半就 _____ 是很难成功的。

Activity 2 Highlight the false description about Mrs. Zhang and then rewrite each sentence in Chinese.

1 张老师在班上**深入**地探讨"民主的精神与价值",最后还**确认**学生都明白了。(hint: 2 mistakes)

_____

2 当张老师一看到晓菲在才艺表演的时候受到干扰,她马上**阻止**了成成和罗雷在教室的起哄和霸凌行为。(hint: 1 mistake)

_____

3 当成成说他要使用他爸爸教的一个招数来**对付**晓菲的时候,张老师马上纠正成成说这并不是一个正确的民主行为。(hint: 2 mistakes)

_____

4 在最后投票结束的场景,张老师跟全班说选举的过程还有经验都不重要,最重要的是大家都拿到了中秋节卡片。(hint: 2 mistakes)

_____

Activity 3 Combine and modify sentence A to E into one coherent chunk.

Eg A 张老师希望三位候选人能**公平**竞争。

  B 张老师希望学生能够学习如何选举。

  C 张老师觉得学生应该利用这次活动来学习什么是民主。

  D 张老师没有注意到三位候选人的资源并不是平等的。

  E 张老师不应该同意罗雷用招待旅游、送礼物的方式来获得支持。

(Answer) 张老师希望三位候选人能公平竞争,利用这次活动来让全班学习如何进行一场民主选举。然而,她并没有注意到三位候选人的资源并不是平等的,她也不应该同意罗雷用招待旅游、送礼物的方式来获得支持。

2 A 张老师是三年级一班的班主任。

  B 张老师在晓菲哭泣的时候鼓励她要勇敢。

  C 张老师在成成想放弃的时候让他回家跟妈妈沟通。

（续表）

D 张老师没有拒绝罗雷父母安排的轻轨旅游。

E 张老师没有说明：选举应该保持**公正**、公平的态度，不能利诱别人，因为这样会形成"贿选"的**风气**。

_____

_____

_____

_____

Activity 4 In the documentary, *Please Vote for Me*, Mrs. Zhang's teaching practice is a key focus. Please read the following English passages and translate into Chinese. As a challenge, discuss with your teacher if you have different perspectives before writing down.

Some scenes in the movie reflect issues with Mrs. Zhang's teaching methods and her treatment of students.

Initially, when Mrs. Zhang announced that a democratic election will be carried out in the class, she did not ensure that all students understood the meaning and spirit of a democratic election. As a result, Cheng Cheng had to ask his stepfather about democracy after returning home.

When Luo Lei started performing his talent, Cheng Cheng told Mrs. Zhang at the back of the classroom that he planned to boo Luo Lei, criticising his singing. At that moment, Mrs. Zhang did not immediately point out that such behaviour was not right.

When Cheng Cheng wanted to give up due to the success of Luo Lei's monorail trip, Mrs. Zhang only told him that it's difficult to succeed if one thinks of giving up at the first sign of difficulty. Mrs. Zhang didn't explain that this "giving others benefits" behaviour in an election from Luo Lei is inappropriate.

配角分析：晓菲妈妈

Xiaofei's mother worked as an administrative staff member at the school where this documentary was filmed. Despite the challenging circumstances as a single mother, she provides her daughter with unwavering support, both emotionally and practically. This support extends from maintaining her physical appearance to nurturing her emotional well-being. Although she doesn't provide financial and material support compared to the other two candidates, she offers abundant emotional support. She has also worked hard to raise Xiaofei into a positive and polite child. When she learnt that Xiaofei was preparing for the class election, knowing her daughter's introverted nature, she encouraged Xiaofei to communicate and interact more with her classmates, hoping to gain more support in school.

Xiaofei's fear of public speaking and potential errors were met with comforting words from her mother, instilling in her the confidence to face her imperfections head-on and use them as a learning opportunity. During a challenging incident, her mother acted as a calming presence, reminding Xiaofei to stay true to herself and uphold her beliefs, despite external influences.

In a conversation with the documentary's director, Xiaofei's mother expressed a degree of guilt for not being able to provide a conventional family setting for her daughter, feeling the strain of not being able to offer the same level of support as two-parent families might.

Ahead of a crucial debate, she took Xiaofei to the park for a relaxing walk, using the opportunity to educate her about the nature of debates and the importance of persuasion over conflict. She gently guided her daughter to think logically and prepare effectively. She also urged Xiaofei to collaborate with her friends to gather crucial information for the debate.

Xiaofei's mother made a conscious decision to take a step back from the election campaign, choosing to assist only in speech-writing while respecting her daughter's thoughts and individuality. This reflects her belief that the educational and growth opportunities the election process offers, outweigh the importance of the final result.

Activity 1 **Based on the film, choose the most appropriate word in the box to fill in the blanks.**

| Ⓐ 安慰 | Ⓑ 温和 | Ⓒ 过程 | Ⓓ 离婚 | Ⓔ 吵架 | Ⓕ 思考 |

1 由于 _____ 的原因，我们可以从纪录片中看到晓菲的妈妈独自一人辛苦地照顾晓菲。

2 晓菲的妈妈把晓菲教导成一个又 _____ 又有礼貌的小孩子。

3 在发生"打倒晓菲"事件的时候，晓菲的妈妈 _____ 正在哭的女儿，并且告诉她不要管别人怎么讲，要勇敢做自己觉得对的事。

4 在准备辩论之前，晓菲的妈妈带她去公园一边散步，一边跟她说辩论不是 _____ ，要以理服人 。

5 晓菲的妈妈耐心地教导女儿要**理性**地 _____ ，做好万全的准备。

6 晓菲的妈妈看重的是选举的 _____ 给女儿带来的成长经验，而不是结果。

以理服人：指通过讲道理的方式来说服他人，让别人接受自己的意见。

Activity 2 Highlight the false description about Xiaofei's mother and then rewrite each sentence in Chinese.

1 晓菲的妈妈是纪录片中学校里的班主任。(hint: 1 mistake)

_____

2 在访谈中，晓菲的妈妈跟导演表示在这次选举中她想多帮帮她女儿，因为她觉得女儿还很小，无法独立面对一些事情。(hint: 2 mistakes)

_____

3 晓菲的妈妈鼓励晓菲去找张老师，帮忙**搜集**其他家长的缺点来当作辩论时的**证据**。(hint: 2 mistakes)

_____

4 晓菲的妈妈想尽办法帮女儿拉票。在跟女儿沟通完之后，除了帮她准备中秋节卡片以外，还按照她的想法与性格，帮她写了演讲稿。(hint: 2 mistakes)

_____

Activity 3 Combine and modify sentence A to E into one coherent chunk.

1 | A 晓菲的妈妈知道女儿要准备班长选举。

B 晓菲的妈妈知道女儿的性格内向。

C 晓菲的妈妈鼓励她跟班上的同学多沟通。

D 晓菲的妈妈希望她跟班上的同学多交流。

E 晓菲的妈妈期待女儿在班上能获得更多人的支持。

_____

_____

_____

_____

2   A 晓菲的妈妈发现女儿非常害怕演讲时出错。

B 妈妈鼓励晓菲时说："说错了又怎样？"

C 晓菲的妈妈期待她可以 独当一面 。

D 晓菲的妈妈期待她勇敢地面对自己的**不足**。

E 晓菲的妈妈期待她成长。

独当一面：形容一个人不需要依靠他人的支持或帮助，自己可以独立解决问题。

Activity 4

In the documentary, *Please Vote for Me*, the interaction and support between Xiaofei's mother and her daughter are key focuses. Please read the following English passages and translate into Chinese. As a challenge, discuss with your teacher if you have different perspectives before writing down.

Xiaofei's mother not only frequently helps tidy up her daughter's hair and appearance, but also provides a warm home. Because she works as an administrative staff member at the school, she can support Xiaofei both inside and outside of school.

Compared to other candidates, Xiaofei's mother may not provide material support, but she offers a lot of emotional encouragement to her daughter.

As a single mother, she often blames herself for not being able to provide her daughter with a complete family and for not being able to comprehensively support her child as other parents might.

配角分析：罗雷父母

Luo Lei's parents, who both work for the police, were keen to support him when they discovered he was running for class monitor. Despite Luo Lei's confidence in managing the campaign on his own, his parents were sceptical and suggested strategies for the election from the beginning. They held high standards for Luo Lei and were often critical of him, as demonstrated by his mother's stringent critique of his flute playing.

Upon discovering Luo Lei's struggle in the campaign, particularly after he was jeered during a talent performance, they decided to intervene. They resorted to bribery, mending Luo Lei's strained relationships with classmates by treating them to a trip on the modern monorail, which has a close connection with his father's workplace. His father also assumed the role of a guide during the trip, educating the students about the city's landmarks.

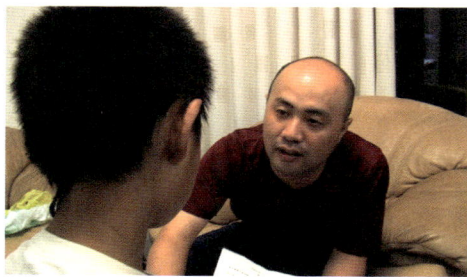

In preparation for the political battleground, they coached Luo Lei on speech modulation and handling counterargument, fabricating unanswerable dilemmas to put his opponents at a disadvantage. Anticipating criticisms about Luo

Lei's strict management style, they trained him to justify it as necessary for maintaining order. They went as far as suggesting that physical punishment could be an appropriate disciplinary measure, an idea that his father reinforced by implying that misbehaving children deserved such punishment.

As a concluding strategy, they prepared gifts for Luo Lei to distribute and extend Mid-Autumn Festival wishes following his campaign speech. They believed this gesture would win the hearts and votes of his classmates.

Activity 1 Based on the film, choose the most appropriate word in the box to fill in the blanks.

> Ⓐ 依靠　　Ⓑ 语气　　Ⓒ 技巧　　Ⓓ 辩论　　Ⓔ 决定　　Ⓕ 设计

1 一开始，罗雷的父母就想说服罗雷选举要使用 ＿＿＿＿＿＿ 。

2 罗雷在才艺表演的**环节**失利之后，他的父母就 ＿＿＿＿＿＿ 出手干预班长选举了。

3 罗雷的父母相信 ＿＿＿＿＿＿ 外在的力量可以帮助自己的小孩儿选上班长。

4 罗雷父亲教罗雷演讲时应注意 ＿＿＿＿＿＿ 的 抑扬顿挫 。

5 罗雷父亲教罗雷在 ＿＿＿＿＿＿ 时如何反击成成。

6 罗雷的父母帮罗雷 ＿＿＿＿＿＿ 了一个**两难**的问题，用来考成成。

抑扬顿挫： 形容人在表达时有节奏感，说话时生动、有魅力。

Activity 2 Highlight the false description about Luo Lei's parents. Rewrite each sentence in Chinese.

1 罗雷的父母都在电视台上班，跟轻轨的单位不熟。(hint: 2 mistakes)

＿＿＿＿＿＿＿＿＿＿＿＿＿＿＿＿＿＿＿＿＿＿＿＿＿＿＿＿＿＿＿＿＿＿＿

2 当罗雷跟父母说不需要他们帮忙的时候，他们露出了生气的表情，因为他们认为儿子可能会去贿赂别人。(hint: 2 mistakes)

_____

3 罗雷的父母一知道儿子要竞选班长就立刻拒绝提供帮助，因为他们希望儿子能够靠自己。(hint: 2 mistakes)

_____

4 罗雷的妈妈在整个火车旅游中充当导游，除了拍照，她还向全班同学演唱了《童话》。(hint: 3 mistakes)

_____

Activity 3 Combine and modify sentence A to E into one coherent chunk.

1   A 罗雷的父母知道罗雷要竞选班长。

B 罗雷的父母想帮罗雷得到更多同学的支持。

C 罗雷告诉父母不需要他们的帮助。

D 罗雷的父母露出了 半信半疑 的表情。

E 罗雷的父母不太相信自己儿子的实力。

_____

_____

_____

_____

2   A 罗雷的父母对罗雷有很高的期望。

B 罗雷的父母对罗雷很严格。

C 罗雷的妈妈在罗雷在练习**长笛**的时候走进他的房间。

D 罗雷的妈妈骂他吹长笛吹得不好，说他吹得"曲不成调"。

E 罗雷的父母似乎只能看到罗雷的缺点，对他缺乏爱与鼓励。

3 A 罗雷的父母猜到有人会不相信自己儿子的管理方式。

B 罗雷的父母猜到有人会用"打人"来作为攻击罗雷的理由。

C 罗雷的父母教罗雷：管理就是要严格，如果不严格，就没有人会听班长的。

D 罗雷的父母义正词严地说："很多大人也会打小孩儿"。

E 罗雷的父母似乎向罗雷传达了"打人是正确的"观念。

半信半疑：有些相信，又有点儿怀疑。

曲不成调：字面意思是指一首曲子跑调了，一般用来形容事情不协调，缺乏一致性或连贯性。

Activity 4

In the documentary, *Please Vote for Me*, the interaction between Luo Lei's parents and their son, and their involvement in his election, are key focuses. Please read the following English passages and translate into Chinese. As a challenge, discuss with your teacher if you have different perspectives before writing down.

We can easily see that Luo Lei's parents influenced their son's election because they have high expectations for him. They reminded him from the start that he needs to use certain strategies to win the election.

To improve Luo Lei's relationship with his classmates, they adopted the method of bribery. They used their work connections to organise a monorail trip, telling Luo Lei to invite his classmates.

In the end, Luo Lei's father also prepared Mid-Autumn Festival cards for his son to distribute before voting. These benefits not only won the hearts of his classmates but also got their votes.

配角分析：成成的妈妈与继父

Cheng Cheng's mother works at a TV station and his stepfather is an engineer. They are highly involved in his daily life, collecting him from school, preparing his meals, and assisting him getting his pyjamas on. When they learnt Cheng Cheng had become one of the candidates for class monitor, his mother enthusiastically supported him, even teaching him how to project his voice while singing, using her professional expertise. However, Cheng Cheng showed more interest in watching TV, which his mother tolerated, showing a degree of indulgence. However, this leniency is overshadowed by instances where Cheng Cheng shows disrespect towards his parents, raising his voice at them and pushing his mother away. Nonetheless, his parents maintain a supportive attitude, continuously praising and encouraging him, leading to Cheng Cheng freely sharing his school experiences with them.

The documentary reveals that Cheng Cheng's parents harbour great expectations for him. When Cheng Cheng showed signs of giving up, his mother insisted that he couldn't as they had the firm belief that success would bring honour to their family, drawing parallels with China's leader, Hu Jintao's early steps. They also guided him at home, proposing strategies such as expressing his intention to be a class monitor promoting harmony, rather than a dictator. His stepfather helped him draft a speech, which his mother, however, perceived as too adult-like. All this immersion and unwavering support meant that Cheng Cheng came to expect his parents' actions as given, contributing to his pampered behaviour.

Activity 1 Based on the film, choose the most appropriate word in the box to fill in the blanks.

> **A** 似乎   **B** 专长   **C** 竞选   **D** 责骂   **E** 记住   **F** 严肃

1 在知道成成要 _____ 班长以后，他的妈妈全力支持他。

2 成成的妈妈想尽办法用自己的 _____ 教成成唱歌。

3 成成喜欢 讨价还价 地跟妈妈说要看电视，但是他的妈妈 _____ 是一个很宠小孩儿的人，没有不准他看。

4 我们也在一些镜头里看到成成对父母没大没小，对他们大呼小叫，甚至在客厅里**粗鲁**地推妈妈，却没有看到他父母大声地 _____ 他。

5 当成成想要放弃时，妈妈 _____ 地回应说他不能够退选，因为他们认为当上班长不仅是一种**荣誉**，也是成为像中国领导人胡锦涛那样的人的第一步。

6 成成的妈妈希望他能够 _____ 班长和同学应该友好相处。

讨价还价： 形容在交易或谈判中双方互相讨论，来达成双方都能接受的结果。

Activity 2 Highlight the false description about Cheng Cheng's parents and then rewrite each sentence in Chinese.

1 成成的妈妈在学校工作，他的继父是一位警察。(hint: 2 mistakes)

2 从纪录片中我们可以发现成成的父母对他有很高的期望，所以安排了轻轨旅游，还给全班同学送礼物。(hint: 2 mistakes)

Activity 3 Combine and modify sentence A to E into one coherent chunk.

---

1   A 成成的父母在日常生活中为他准备**饭菜**。

B 成成的父母帮他换上睡衣。

C 成成的父母放学后在校门口接他。

D 成成的父母**尽量**满足他生活上的需求。

E 成成的父母给了成成很多**亲情**和爱。

---

2   A 成成的父母在生活上为他做了很多事情。

B 成成的父母挺宠小孩儿的。

C 成成觉得父母为自己做事是 理所当然 的。

D 成成常常在家对父母没大没小的。

E 成成养成了**骄纵**的性格。

理所当然：指事物符合情理，没有什么值得惊讶或质疑的。

Activity 4 In the documentary, *Please Vote for Me,* the interaction between Cheng Cheng's parents and their son, as well as how they assist him in the election, are key focuses. Please read the following English passages and translate into Chinese. As a challenge, discuss with your teacher if you have different perspectives before writing down.

Cheng Cheng's parents have high expectations for him, hoping he will become someone as famous as Hu Jintao in the future.

They always encourage him, often telling him that he is the best, which is why Cheng Cheng enjoys talking to them and sharing what happens at school.

Cheng Cheng's mother continuously helped her son at home throughout this election. For instance, she taught him how to use "Chi" to sing and advised him to tell the class that he wants to be a manager of the class, not a ruler.

Cheng Cheng's stepfather also helped him write a speech, even though the content is written in an adult's voice, which may not be understood by children.

<table>
<tr><td></td><td></td><td></td><td></td><td></td><td></td><td></td><td></td><td></td></tr>
<tr><td></td><td></td><td></td><td></td><td></td><td></td><td></td><td></td><td></td></tr>
<tr><td></td><td></td><td></td><td></td><td></td><td></td><td></td><td></td><td></td></tr>
<tr><td></td><td></td><td></td><td></td><td></td><td></td><td></td><td></td><td></td></tr>
</table>

(Extension) 根据你学到的内容，讨论下面的问题。

1 说一说他们每个人的行为和性格特点？

2 纪录片中哪些场景展现了以上特点？

3 身为大人，家长们对这场小孩儿的选举抱着什么样的期待？

4 对于这场民主选举，家长各自有什么样的信念／想法？

5 家长的行为、背景和知识是如何影响三位候选人的？

Chapter

5

Essay Practice

In this chapter, there are a series of questions for essay practice. Additionally, we provide content prompts and guidelines that students can refer to when answering these questions. Please ensure that students carefully review the following key points in writing and utilise the English checklist to assist in their writing process.

写作重点提醒

写作前

- 先仔细阅读作文题目。读懂题目后，圈出其中的关键词。
- 计划作文中的三个部分：开头（introduction）、主体（main body）和结论（conclusion）。
- 针对主体部分，利用关键词想出跟题目有关的三个观点。
- 想一想电影中有哪些证据和例子可以用来支持你的观点。
- 想一想电影中有哪些议题、主题和社会历史背景跟你的观点相关。

写作时

内容

- 在主体部分，至少阐述三个观点，一个观点为一个段落。
- 每个段落的长度尽量差不多，而且主要的观点不重复。
- 在每一个段落的开头，用一两句话当作"主题句"来清楚地告诉读者你的观点（**P**oint）：破题法。
- 在每一个段落，你能从影片中找出相关的例子（**E**xample）或证据（**E**vidence）来支持你的观点。
- 在每一个段落，你能根据这部电影的人物、情节、场景、语言、主题、文化现象、社会背景或拍摄手法，来进行相关性和批判性分析（**A**nalysis）。
- 在每一个段落的最后，你能够把你的分析连接（**L**ink）到你自己的观点或导演拍摄这部纪录片的目的。
- 为了充分回答考试的问题，你的作文要尽量达到或超过考试要求的字数。
- 作文最后的结论必须呼应题目，不能有新的观点。

语言

- 使用 A Level 高级语法、句型、词语及合适的成语。
- 多用同义词，避免重复使用同样的字词。
- 写作后注意检查句型和语法。
- 避免汉字及语法错误。

Essay Writing Checklist

Before you hand in your essay, ensure you've gone through each of these steps:

Before Starting the Essay

- ☐ I have understood the question and circled the keywords.
- ☐ I have planned the three main parts of my essay: introduction, main body, and conclusion.
- ☐ I have brainstormed three analytical and convincing points of view related to the question and noted them down as keywords.
- ☐ I have considered how my viewpoints relate to the topics, themes, and historical and social backgrounds of the film.
- ☐ I have considered which themes, topics and evidence from the film can best support my arguments.

During Writing the Essay

Content

- ☐ My introduction clearly states the main point(s) that I am going to discuss.
- ☐ I have produced at least three coherent paragraphs in the main body, discussing one relevant viewpoint in each paragraph.
- ☐ I have one or two topic sentences to clearly introduce my point at the beginning of each paragraph.
- ☐ I have ensured all my points address the essay question and used relevant examples as evidence from the film to support them.
- ☐ I have used my knowledge of the characters, plot, settings, language, themes, cultural and social background, or cinematography in the film to produce a critical analysis for each of my points.
- ☐ At the end of each paragraph, I have linked my analysis to my viewpoint or to the director's purpose for making the documentary.
- ☐ I have attempted to maintain a consistent paragraph length and ensured the main points in each paragraph are valid and not repetitive.
- ☐ My conclusion directly addresses the essay question and does not introduce any new ideas.
- ☐ My essay goes beyond the required word count to adequately answer the exam question.

Language

- ☐ I have incorporated A Level advanced grammar, diverse sentence structures, appropriate vocabulary, and relevant idioms.

☐ I have used synonyms correctly to avoid repetition.

☐ After writing, I have checked my essay for sentence structure and grammar.

☐ I have been careful to avoid frequent mistakes in Chinese characters and other grammatical errors.

Essay Questions

1 讨论《请投我一票》中哪些场景表现了有中国特色的校园文化。

2 讨论纪录片《请投我一票》中导演常用的摄影技巧及其用意。

3 三位学生对于自己成为班长候选人之后的态度及表现各不相同，请对比讨论。

4 比较三位候选人在班长选举过程中每个阶段的转变。

5 分析三位候选人的性格差异。

6 比较三位候选人与各自家人的关系有何差异。

7 讨论纪录片《请投我一票》中大人的行为对选举和三位候选人产生的影响。

8 分析罗雷最后为什么赢得了班长选举。

9 导演是如何提醒观众三位候选人仍然是孩子的？

10 讨论晓菲在班长选举中遭遇的困难以及她是如何克服这些困难的。

11 分析班上其他同学在班长选举过程中起到的作用。

12 讨论这场民主班长选举面临的问题及挑战。

Appendix I
Guidance for Chapter 5 Essay Questions

Each question provides suggested guiding questions to help you brainstorm answers. Your answers should not be limited tc the guiding questions.

1 讨论《请投我一票》中哪些场景表现了有中国特色的校园文化。

Discuss which scenes in *Please Vote for Me* demonstrate the unique characteristics of Chinese school culture.

(1) What do you think about the flag-raising ceremony? Is there a special item which all students wear?

(2) What do you think about students singing patriotic songs and decorating classrooms with the Chinese flag and slogans?

(3) What is your view on students reading aloud together in class during some scenes?

(4) What do you think about the whole-school exercise sessions during breaks?

2 讨论纪录片《请投我一票》中导演常用的摄影技巧及其用意。

Discuss the cinematographic techniques frecuently used by the director in the film *Please Vote for Me* and their purposes.

(1) What is your view on the close-up shots used in the film? Please provide examples.

(2) What is your view on the medium shot used in the film? Please provide examples.

(3) What are the significant meanings and effects of using montage? Why does the director use montage for some parts of the film? Give examples.

3 三位学生对于自己成为班长候选人之后的态度以及表现各不相同，请对比讨论。

The three candidates exhibit different attitudes and behaviours upon becoming candidates for class monitor. Please discuss.

(1) Based on your observations, what was Cheng Cheng's reaction when he learned that he was going to participate in a democratic election? How much does he know about the meaning of "democracy"? Was he prepared to campaign?

(2) What was Luo Lei's reaction when it was announced that he was one of the chosen candidates? What was his attitude when he told his parents about this news at home?

(3) How did Xiaofei react when she first learned that she had become one of the candidates? Upon returning home, what are your thoughts on the interaction between her and her mother?

4 比较三位候选人在班长选举过程中每个阶段的转变。

Compare the transformation of the three candidates at each stage of the class monitor election process.

(1) What are your thoughts on Cheng Cheng's understanding of participating in a democratic election throughout the film? What tactics and strategies did he employ at each stage? Do you believe he remained consistent or was influenced over as the film progressed?

(2) What were Luo Lei's initial beliefs upon learning he would participate in the election? How did he approach facing challenges, and to what extent did he change?

(3) What is your perspective on Xiaofei's transformation from preparing for the talent show with her mother at the beginning to her final speech throughout the film?

5 分析三位候选人的性格差异。

Analyse the personalities of the three candidates.

(1) What do you think of Xiaofei's personality? Does it affect her performance in the election? Have you noticed any changes in her

throughout the electoral process?

(2) What do you think of Cheng Cheng's personality? Does it afford him various advantages during the election? How do you view the impact of his personality on his behaviour at home and in school?

(3) What do you think about Luo Lei's personality? Do you believe the parenting he has experienced could potentially influence his character development? How do you perceive his personality or behaviour affecting his relationship with his classmates?

6 比较三位候选人与各自家人的关系有何差异。

Compare the relationships of the three candidates with their families.

(1) What are your thoughts on the parenting in Cheng Cheng's family? How do you perceive the interactions between Cheng Cheng and his mother at home? What is his mum's expectation of Cheng Cheng?

(2) What are your thoughts on the parenting in Luo Lei's family? How do you perceive the interactions between Luo Lei's parents and their son and how they interfered in the election to show their support?

(3) How does Xiaofei's mum look after her daughter? What is the relationship like between Xiaofei and her mother in various scenes? Are there any differences compared to the other two candidates' families?

7 讨论纪录片《请投我一票》中大人的行为对选举和三位候选人产生的影响。

Discuss the impact of the adults' behaviour in the film *Please Vote for Me* on the election and the three candidates.

(1) What are your thoughts on how the form tutor (Mrs. Zhang) explains the meaning of a democratic election?

(2) What is you view on Mrs. Zhang's reaction when Cheng Cheng told her about the tactics to undermine Luo Lei's performance in the talent show?

(3) What is your view on Luo Lei's parents organising a monorail trip and later giving the Mid-Autumn Festival gifts to support their son?

(4) How do you view the ways in which all three candidates' parents assist with writing their speeches?

8 分析罗雷最后为什么赢得了班长选举。

Analyse why Luo Lei won the election in the end.

(1) What advantages does Luo Lei have from being a class monitor for several years?

(2) How do you view Luo Lei's personality and his approach to the election?

(3) How did he prepare for and perform in the talent show, debates, and the final speech?

(4) Do you think Xiaofei and Cheng Cheng were competitive enough to be his rivals?

(5) What is your view on the intervention by Luo Lei's parents throughout the election?

9 导演是如何提醒观众三位候选人仍然是孩子的？

How does the director remind the audience that the three candidates are still children?

(1) How do we see the three candidates express their emotions openly during the film?

(2) Do the three candidates lack the ability to distinguish right from wrong, and how are they easily influenced by others' words and actions?

(3) How does the director interweave scenes of the candidates participating in school activities, showing that they still have duties and responsibilities as students?

(4) What shots highlight the three candidates' innocent nature and behaviour?

10 讨论晓菲在班长选举中遭遇的困难以及她是如何克服这些困难的。

Discuss the challenges Xiaofei faced during the class monitor election and how she overcame them.

(1) How did Xiaofei manage the interruption in her talent show performance?

(2) What other challenges did she face at different stages of the campaign?

(3) What are your thoughts on how Xiaofei responded to her loss in the election after Luo Lei's decisive victory?

11 分析班上其他同学在班长选举过程中起到的作用。

Analyse the role of the classmates in the class monitor election and its underlying significance.

(1) How did the participation of the candidates' helpers contribute to the unfolding of the election?

(2) Why did the director interview students about their preferred candidates?

(3) What is your perspective on whether the director intentionally or unintentionally depicted these classmates as resembling real-world voters?

12 讨论这场民主班长选举面临的问题及挑战。

Discuss the challenges and issues faced in this class monitor's election.

(1) How did the disparity in family backgrounds influence the performance and outcome of the election for the three candidates?

(2) How did the unclear election rules affect the fairness of the election?

(3) How did the negative and unfair tactics pervade the election?

Appendix II
Vocabulary

Chapter 2 Unit 1

中文	拼音	英文
著名	zhùmíng	
纪录片	jìlùpiàn	
导演	dǎoyǎn	
由于	yóuyú	
摄影	shèyǐng	
技巧	jìqiǎo	
社会	shèhuì	
探讨	tàntǎo	
近年来	jìnnián lái	
受到	shòudào	
关注	guānzhù	
作品	zuòpǐn	
主题	zhǔtí	
大多	dàduō	
来自	láizì	
题材	tícái	
例如	lìrú	
现实	xiànshí	
尊重	zūnzhòng	
拍摄	pāishè	
中心思想	zhōngxīn sīxiǎng	
表现出	biǎoxiànchū	
强烈	qiángliè	
责任感	zérèngǎn	

* 查找词典，填写生词表中的英文部分。

中文	拼音	英文
真实	zhēnshí	
竞选	jìngxuǎn	
班长	bānzhǎng	
过程	guòchéng	
获得	huòdé	
奖	jiǎng	
偶然	ǒurán	
机会	jīhuì	
同事	tóngshì	
领导	lǐngdǎo	
批改	pīgǎi	
辛苦	xīnkǔ	
失败	shībài	
于是	yúshì	
调查	diàochá	
发现	fāxiàn	
感到	gǎndào	
职业	zhíyè	
决定	juédìng	
原因	yuányīn	
手法	shǒufǎ	
感受	gǎnshòu	
激烈	jīliè	
选举	xuǎnjǔ	
呈现	chéngxiàn	
教育	jiàoyù	
大众	dàzhòng	

中文	拼音	英文
了解	liǎojiě	

Chapter 2 Unit 2

中文	拼音	英文
拥有	yōngyǒu	
丰富	fēngfù	
比较	bǐjiào	
金融中心	jīnróng zhōngxīn	
高等学校	gāoděng xuéxiào	
世纪	shìjì	
经济	jīngjì	
发展	fāzhǎn	
进行	jìnxíng	
方面	fāngmiàn	
完整	wánzhěng	
铁路	tiělù	
网络	wǎngluò	
运输	yùnshū	
高架	gāojià	
路线	lùxiàn	
完工	wángōng	
除此以外	chúcǐ yǐwài	
使用	shǐyòng	
公共	gōnggòng	
智能	zhìnéng	
电动	diàndòng	
轻轨	qīngguǐ	

中文	拼音	英文
现代	xiàndài	
父母	fùmǔ	
乘坐	chéngzuò	
流露出	liúlùchū	
兴奋	xīngfèn	
表情	biǎoqíng	

Chapter 2 Unit 3

中文	拼音	英文
基础	jīchǔ	
培养	péiyǎng	
学习	xuéxí	
知识	zhīshi	
通过	tōngguò	
课程	kèchéng	
技能	jìnéng	
注重	zhùzhòng	
提升	tíshēng	
创新	chuàngxīn	
批判	pīpàn	
思维	sīwéi	
团队	tuánduì	
合作	hézuò	
学校	xuéxiào	
尽力	jìnlì	
提供	tígōng	

中文	拼音	英文
资源	zīyuán	
多元化	duōyuánhuà	
鼓励	gǔlì	
家长	jiāzhǎng	
积极	jījí	
支持	zhīchí	
辅导	fǔdǎo	
甚至	shènzhì	
安排	ānpái	
才艺	cáiyì	
之一	zhī yī	
表达	biǎodá	
写作	xiězuò	
场景	chǎngjǐng	
关于	guānyú	
演讲	yǎnjiǎng	
文章	wénzhāng	
重视	zhòngshì	
认为	rènwéi	
一部分	yí bùfen	
标志	biāozhì	
代表	dàibiǎo	
勇敢	yǒnggǎn	
象征	xiàngzhēng	
伟大	wěidà	
佩戴	pèidài	
意识	yìshí	

中文	拼音	英文
观察	guānchá	
自觉	zìjué	
表现	biǎoxiàn	
精神	jīngshén	
细节	xìjié	
情感	qínggǎn	

Chapter 2 Unit 4

中文	拼音	英文
家庭	jiātíng	
富有	fùyǒu	
一般来说	yìbān lái shuō	
生活	shēnghuó	
水平	shuǐpíng	
地位	dìwèi	
财富	cáifù	
某些	mǒuxiē	
情况	qíngkuàng	
关系	guānxì	
得到	dédào	
优势	yōushì	
人生	rénshēng	
取得	qǔdé	
背景	bèijǐng	
并	bìng	
国家	guójiā	

中文	拼音	英文
展现	zhǎnxiàn	
利用	lìyòng	
工作	gōngzuò	
单位	dānwèi	
方法	fāngfǎ	
赢	yíng	
提高	tígāo	
辩论	biànlùn	
准备	zhǔnbèi	
重点	zhòngdiǎn	
训练	xùnliàn	
如何	rúhé	
所有	suǒyǒu	
倾尽全力	qīngjìn-quánlì	
面对	miànduì	
天壤之别	tiānrǎngzhībié	
单亲	dānqīn	
性格	xìnggé	
内向	nèixiàng	
意见	yìjiàn	
访谈	fǎngtán	
条件	tiáojiàn	
觉得	juéde	
无法	wúfǎ	
期望	qīwàng	
管理	guǎnlǐ	
事	shì	

中文	拼音	英文
思考	sīkǎo	
平衡	pínghéng	

Chapter 2 Unit 5

中文	拼音	英文
霸凌	bàlíng	
暴力	bàolì	
危害	wēihài	
未来	wèilái	
人际关系	rénjì guānxì	
造成	zàochéng	
影响	yǐngxiǎng	
种类	zhǒnglèi	
包括	bāokuò	
职位	zhíwèi	
骂	mà	
方式	fāngshì	
使	shǐ	
根据	gēnjù	
事件	shìjiàn	
不了了之	bùliǎo-liǎozhī	
主要	zhǔyào	
抱	bào	
大事化小，小事化了	dàshì huà xiǎo, xiǎoshì huà liǎo	
处理	chùlǐ	

中文	拼音	英文
态度	tàidù	
及时	jíshí	
表演	biǎoyǎn	
立刻	lìkè	
清楚	qīngchǔ	
专业	zhuānyè	

Chapter 2 Unit 6

中文	拼音	英文
独生子女	dúshēng-zǐnǚ	
政策	zhèngcè	
政府	zhèngfǔ	
计划生育	jìhuà shēngyù	
提倡	tíchàng	
夫妇	fūfù	
目的	mùdì	
追求	zhuīqiú	
降低	jiàngdī	
人口	rénkǒu	
增长	zēngzhǎng	
带来	dàilái	
压力	yālì	
防止	fángzhǐ	
面临	miànlín	
人民	rénmín	
然而	rán'ér	

中文	拼音	英文
长期	chángqī	
措施	cuòshī	
缓解	huǎnjiě	
对于	duìyú	
不一定	bù yídìng	
挑战	tiǎozhàn	
克服	kèfú	
困难	kùnnán	
超出	chāochū	
想象	xiǎngxiàng	
研究	yánjiū	
提到	tídào	
缺乏	quēfá	
兄弟姐妹	xiōngdì jiěmèi	
互动	hùdòng	
沟通	gōutōng	
经验	jīngyàn	
导致	dǎozhì	
陪伴	péibàn	
孤独	gūdú	
尤其	yóuqí	
聚会	jùhuì	
独立	dúlì	
唯一	wéiyī	
竞争	jìngzhēng	
祖父母	zǔ fùmǔ	
养老	yǎnglǎo	

中文	拼音	英文
养育	yǎngyù	
比例	bǐlì	
严重	yánzhòng	
传宗接代	chuánzōng-jiēdài	
观念	guānniàn	
根深蒂固	gēnshēn-dìgù	
数量	shùliàng	
限制	xiànzhì	
结构	jiégòu	
宠坏	chǒnghuài	
镜头	jìngtóu	
展露无遗	zhǎnlù-wúyí	
依赖	yīlài	
目中无人	mùzhōng-wúrén	
结束	jiéshù	
法律	fǎlù	
允许	yǔnxǔ	
仍然	réngrán	

Chapter 2 Unit 7

中文	拼音	英文
多党	duōdǎng	
政治	zhèngzhì	
协商	xiéshāng	
执政党	zhízhèng dǎng	
民主	mínzhǔ	

中文	拼音	英文
党派	dǎngpài	
参与	cānyǔ	
讨论	tǎolùn	
事务	shìwù	
体现	tǐxiàn	
制度	zhìdù	
西方	xīfāng	
系统	xìtǒng	
特色	tèsè	
标准	biāozhǔn	
真正	zhēnzhèng	
意义	yìyì	
纠正	jiūzhèng	
联想	liánxiǎng	
是否	shìfǒu	
暗示	ànshì	
品格	pǐngé	
能够	nénggòu	

Chapter 2 Unit 8

中文	拼音	英文
成为	chéngwéi	
改革	gǎigé	
推行	tuīxíng	
进步	jìnbù	
时期	shíqī	

中文	拼音	英文
国内	guónèi	
增长率	zēngzhǎng lǜ	
周边	zhōubiān	
贸易	màoyì	
增强	zēngqiáng	
和谐	héxié	
世界	shìjiè	
平等	píngděng	
开放	kāifàng	
稳定	wěndìng	
解决	jiějué	
就业	jiùyè	
可持续	kěchíxù	
用心良苦	yòngxīn-liángkǔ	
体会	tǐhuì	
优秀	yōuxiù	
比喻	bǐyù	
意思	yìsi	

Chapter 2 Unit 9

中文	拼音	英文
犯罪	fànzuì	
利益	lìyì	
作为	zuòwéi	
效率	xiàolǜ	
形象	xíngxiàng	

中文	拼音	英文
记录	jìlù	
反映	fǎnyìng	
竭尽所能	jiéjìn-suǒnéng	
邀请	yāoqǐng	
拿出	náchū	
耳提面命	ěrtí-miànmìng	
间接	jiànjiē	
不择手段	bùzé-shǒuduàn	
现象	xiànxiàng	

Chapter 3 Unit 1

中文	拼音	英文
回答	huídá	
爱国励志	àiguó lìzhì	
自强不息	zìqiáng-bùxī	
冉冉升起	rǎnrǎn shēngqǐ	
采访	cǎifǎng	
近距离	jìn jùlí	
面部	miànbù	
直接	zhíjiē	
天真	tiānzhēn	
严肃	yánsù	
形成	xíngchéng	
整齐划一	zhěngqí-huàyī	
画面	huàmiàn	
井然有序	jǐngrán-yǒuxù	
天真无邪	tiānzhēn-wúxié	

中文	拼音	英文
缓缓	huǎnhuǎn	
朝气蓬勃	zhāoqì-péngbó	
相同年龄	xiāngtóng niánlíng	
反复	fǎnfù	
整整齐齐	zhěngzhěng qíqí	
高兴	gāoxìng	

Chapter 3 Unit 2

中文	拼音	英文
要求	yāoqiú	
宣布	xuānbù	
发表	fābiǎo	
陆陆续续	lùlù xùxù	
人物	rénwù	
心不在焉	xīnbú-zàiyān	
视角	shìjiǎo	
身临其境	shēnlínqíjìng	
状况	zhuàngkuàng	
一字排开	yī zì pái kāi	
诚实勇敢	chéngshí yǒnggǎn	
好学多思	hàoxué duōsī	
传达	chuándá	

Chapter 3 Unit 3

中文	拼音	英文
言听计从	yántīng-jìcóng	

中文	拼音	英文
继父	jìfù	
实力	shílì	
控制	kòngzhì	
紧锣密鼓	jǐnluó-mìgǔ	
练习	liànxí	
差异	chāyì	
运用	yùnyòng	
对话	duìhuà	
理解	lǐjiě	
一览无遗	yìlǎn-wúyí	
采用	cǎiyòng	
拒绝	jùjué	
相比	xiāngbǐ	
平淡	píngdàn	
印象	yìnxiàng	

Chapter 3 Unit 4

中文	拼音	英文
伙伴	huǒbàn	
旋律	xuánlǜ	
展示	zhǎnshì	
略胜一筹	luèshèng-yìchóu	
想法	xiǎngfǎ	
起哄	qǐhòng	
手足无措	shǒuzú-wúcuò	
哭	kū	

中文	拼音	英文
只好	zhǐhǎo	
欣赏	xīnshǎng	
赔不是	péi búshi	
整理	zhěnglǐ	
接受	jiēshòu	
完成	wánchéng	
写	xiě	
冲突	chōngtū	
母女	mǔnǚ	
交流	jiāoliú	
若有所思	ruòyǒusuǒsī	
交头接耳	jiāotóu-jiē'ěr	
和平	hépíng	
场面	chǎngmiàn	
紧张	jǐnzhāng	
一群	yì qún	
哭泣	kūqì	
矛盾	máodùn	
满足	mǎnzú	
开玩笑	kāi wánxiào	
转变	zhuǎnbiàn	
爱护	àihù	
缺乏	quēfá	
成长	chéngzhǎng	
愿望	yuànwàng	

Chapter 3 Unit 5

中文	拼音	英文
接着	jiēzhe	
演唱	yǎnchàng	
流行	liúxíng	
空	kōng	
胸有成竹	xiōngyǒu chéngzhú	
气氛	qìfēn	
热闹	rènao	
小型	xiǎoxíng	
演唱会	yǎnchànghuì	
感染	gǎnrǎn	
表示	biǎoshì	
求好心切	qiúhǎo xīnqiè	
一问一答	yí wèn yì dá	
候选人	hòuxuǎnrén	
选民	xuǎnmín	
全景	quánjǐng	
宣传	xuānchuán	
明星	míngxīng	
个人	gèrén	
投入	tóurù	
拍手	pāishǒu	
角度	jiǎodù	
注意	zhùyì	
节目	jiémù	
折射	zhéshè	

中文	拼音	英文
文化	wénhuà	
令	lìng	

Chapter 3 Unit 6

中文	拼音	英文
发生	fāshēng	
善良	shànliáng	
招数	zhāoshù	
批评	pīpíng	
言行	yánxíng	
看起来	kàn qǐlái	
反击	fǎnjī	
反应	fǎnyìng	
忧虑	yōulù	
放弃	fàngqì	
利诱	lìyòu	
认真	rènzhēn	
主角	zhǔjué	
配角	pèijué	
校园	xiàoyuán	
提醒	tíxǐng	
厉害	lìhai	
打扰	dǎrǎo	
另外	lìngwài	
照相机	zhàoxiàngjī	
照片	zhàopiàn	

中文	拼音	英文
恍然大悟	huǎngrán-dàwù	
突然	tūrán	
明白	míngbai	
出现	chūxiàn	
各	gè	
相信	xiāngxìn	
失望	shīwàng	
感动	gǎndòng	

Chapter 3 Unit 7

中文	拼音	英文
建议	jiànyì	
现代化	xiàndàihuà	
借	jiè	
感情	gǎnqíng	
友谊	yǒuyì	
本来	běnlái	
月台	yuètái	
回忆	huíyì	
愉快	yúkuài	
设施	shèshī	
热情	rèqíng	
心中不是滋味	xīnzhōng bú shì zīwèi	
打铁要趁热	dǎtiě yào chènrè	
拉	lā	
献计	xiànjì	

中文	拼音	英文
全力以赴	quánlìyǐfù	
一言不发	yìyán-bùfā	
身体	shēntǐ	
尽心尽力	jìnxīn jìnlì	
转折点	zhuǎnzhé diǎn	
心情	xīnqíng	
建筑物	jiànzhùwù	
拿	ná	
取悦	qǔyuè	
争执	zhēngzhí	
亲密	qīnmì	
特写	tèxiě	
变得	biànde	
烦恼	fánnǎo	
当	dāng	
情节	qíngjié	

Chapter 3 Unit 8

中文	拼音	英文
母亲	mǔqīn	
到来	dàolái	
以理服人	yǐlǐ-fúrén	
尝试	chángshì	
并且	bìngqiě	
访问	fǎngwèn	
重拾信心	chóngshí xìnxīn	

中文	拼音	英文
以身作则	yǐshēn-zuòzé	
作用	zuòyòng	
找	zhǎo	
不切实际	búqiè-shíjì	
谈话	tánhuà	
爱出风头	ài chū fēngtou	
好胜	hàoshèng	
轻松	qīngsōng	
从	cóng	
显示	xiǎnshì	
即将到来	jíjiāng dàolái	
争取	zhēngqǔ	
语气	yǔqì	
言行不一	yánxíng bùyī	
各种	gèzhǒng	
活动	huódòng	
产生	chǎnshēng	
共同	gòngtóng	

Chapter 3 Unit 9

中文	拼音	英文
担心	dānxīn	
无话可说	wúhuà-kěshuō	
纸条	zhǐtiáo	
不同之处	bùtóng zhīchù	
他人	tārén	

中文	拼音	英文
分析	fènxī	
听话	tīnghuà	
针锋相对	zhēnfēng-xiàngduì	
充满	chōngmǎn	
笔记	bǐjì	
偷	tōu	
愿意	yuànyì	
成熟	chéngshú	
陈述	chénshù	
特质	tèzhì	
必须	bìxū	
样子	yàngzi	
有理有据	yǒulǐ yǒujù	

Chapter 3 Unit 10

中文	拼音	英文
演讲稿	yǎnjiǎng gǎo	
安慰	ānwèi	
背	bèi	
手势	shǒushì	
真诚	zhēnchéng	
讲述	jiǎngshù	
出色	chūsè	
回报	huíbào	
截然不同	jiérán-bùtóng	
倍感压力	bèigǎn yālì	

中文	拼音	英文
滚	gǔn	
失控	shīkòng	
势均力敌	shìjūn-lìdí	
道谢	dàoxiè	
最后冲刺	zuìhòu chōngcì	
偶尔	ǒu'ěr	
办公室	bàngōngshì	
按照	ànzhào	
躺	tǎng	
疲劳	píláo	
忘	wàng	

Chapter 3 Unit 11

中文	拼音	英文
规则	guīzé	
选票	xuǎnpiào	
唱票	chàngpiào	
结果	jiéguǒ	
艰苦	jiānkǔ	
握手	wòshǒu	
终于	zhōngyú	
手舞足蹈	shǒuwǔ-zúdǎo	
票房	piàofáng	
小心翼翼	xiǎoxīn-yìyì	
恭喜	gōngxǐ	
骄傲	jiāo'ào	

中文	拼音	英文
毫无掩饰	háowú yǎnshì	
风度	fēngdù	

Chapter 4 Unit 1

中文	拼音	英文
个人信息	gèrén xìnxī	
服装	fúzhuāng	
动机	dòngjī	
显得	xiǎnde	
喝倒彩	hè dàocǎi	
活泼	huópō	
外向	wàixiàng	
害羞	hàixiū	
勇气	yǒngqì	
嘲笑	cháoxiào	
深刻	shēnkè	
在意	zàiyì	
挫折	cuòzhē	
说服	shuōfú	
足够	zúgòu	
干涉	gānshè	
正直	zhèngzhí	
值得	zhídé	
对象	duìxiàng	
善于	shànyú	
主见	zhǔjiàn	
大方	dàfang	

中文	拼音	英文
收集	shōují	
威胁	wēixié	
充分	chōngfèn	
对比	duìbǐ	
确定	quèdìng	
负面	fùmiàn	
坚定	jiāndìng	
经历	jīnglì	
一波三折	yìbō-sānzhé	

Chapter 4 Unit 2

中文	拼音	英文
提出	tíchū	
观众	guānzhòng	
大呼小叫	dàhū-xiǎojiào	
继续	jìxù	
话题	huàtí	
消息	xiāoxi	
功夫	gōngfu	
和睦相处	hémù xiāngchǔ	
统治	tǒngzhì	
能言善道	néngyán shàndào	
输	shū	
道歉	dàoqiàn	
委员	wěiyuán	
权力	quánlì	
干扰	gānrǎo	

中文	拼音	英文
串通	chuàntōng	
故意	gùyì	
带头	dàitóu	
弱点	ruòdiǎn	
策划	cèhuà	
心机	xīnjī	
由此可见	yóu cǐ kějiàn	
教训	jiàoxùn	
比如	bǐrú	
实话	shíhuà	
下降	xiàjiàng	

Chapter 4 Unit 3

中文	拼音	英文
适合	shìhé	
似乎	sìhū	
咄咄逼人	duōduō-bī rén	
退出	tuìchū	
干预	gānyù	
坚持	jiānchí	
光明正大	guāngmíng-zhèngdà	
不可否认	bùkě fǒurèn	
尊敬	zūnjìng	
绝对	juéduì	
潜移默化	qiányí-mòhuà	
义正词严	yìzhèng-cíyán	

中文	拼音	英文
前所未有	qiánsuǒwèiyǒu	
解释	jiěshì	
合理	hélǐ	
体罚	tǐfá	

Chapter 4 Unit 4

中文	拼音	英文
班主任	bānzhǔrèn	
强调	qiángdiào	
权利	quánlì	
深入	shēnrù	
确认	quèrèn	
阻止	zǔzhǐ	
对付	duìfu	
公平	gōngpíng	
公正	gōngzhèng	
风气	fēngqì	

Chapter 4 Unit 5

中文	拼音	英文
温和	wēnhé	
离婚	líhūn	
吵架	chǎojià	
理性	lǐxìng	
搜集	sōují	
证据	zhèngjù	

中文	拼音	英文
独当一面	dúdāng-yímiàn	
不足	bùzú	

Chapter 4 Unit 6

中文	拼音	英文
设计	shèjì	
环节	huánjié	
抑扬顿挫	yìyáng-dùncuò	
两难	liǎngnán	
半信半疑	bànxìn-bànyí	
长笛	chángdí	
曲不成调	qǔ bù chéng diào	

Chapter 4 Unit 7

中文	拼音	英文
专长	zhuāncháng	
责骂	zémà	
记住	jìzhù	
讨价还价	tǎojià-huánjià	
粗鲁	cūlǔ	
荣誉	róngyù	
饭菜	fàncài	
尽量	jǐnliàng	
亲情	qīnqíng	
理所当然	lǐsuǒdāngrán	
骄纵	jiāozòng	